PEGASUS ENCYCLOPEDIA LIBRARY

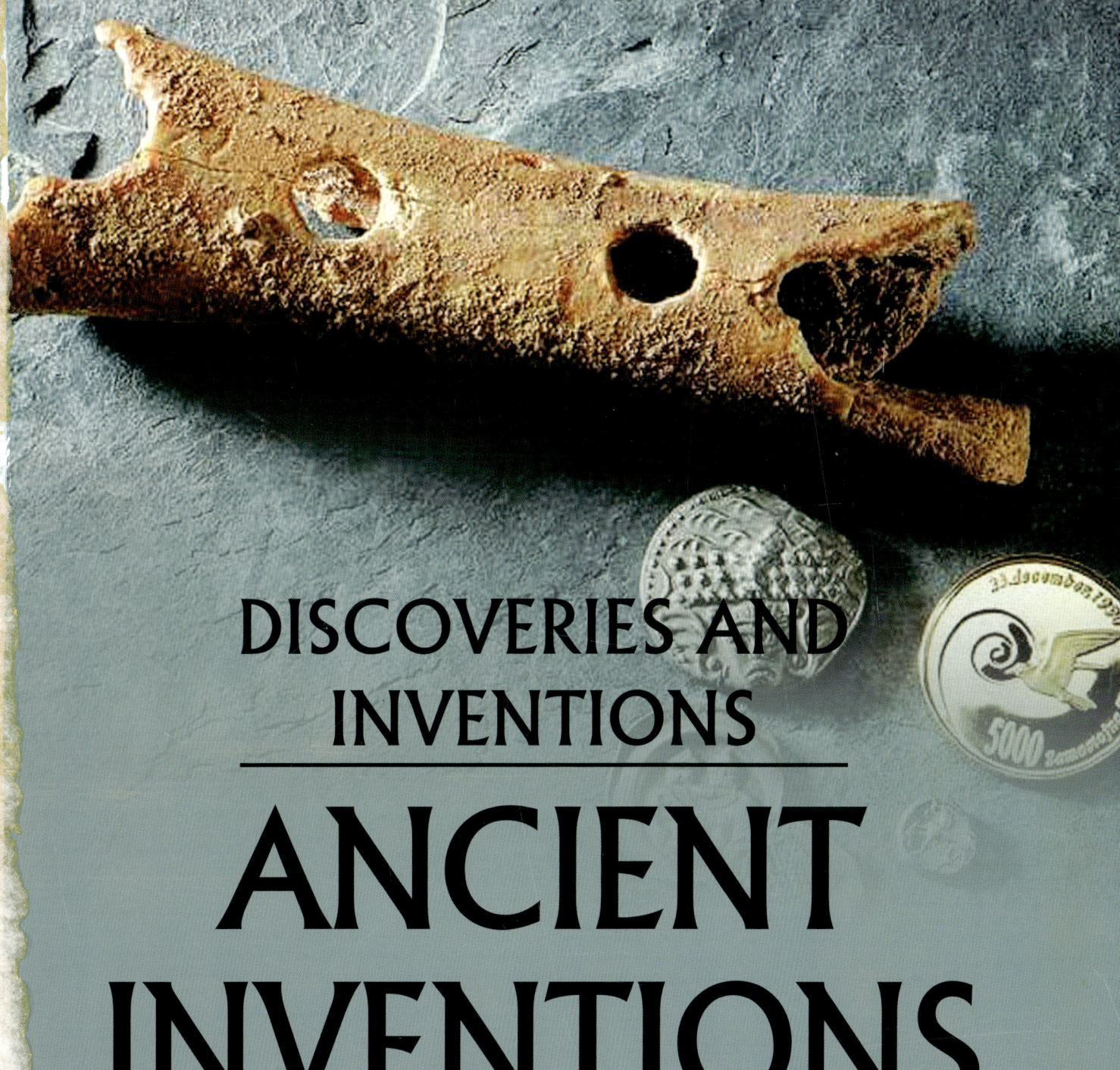

DISCOVERIES AND INVENTIONS
ANCIENT INVENTIONS

Edited by: Anil Kumar Tomar, Pallabi B. Tomar
Managing editor: Tapasi De
Designed by: Vijesh Chahal, Anil Kumar, Rohit Kumar
Illustrated by: Suman S. Roy, Tanoy Choudhury
Colouring done by: Vinay Kumar, Sonu, Kiran Kumari & Pradeep Kumar

CONTENTS

Introduction 3
Making fire 4
Pigments 8
Needle and thread 9
The bow and arrow 10
Musical instruments 12
The boat 13
Clothing 14
Animal domestication 15
Ropes 17
Agriculture 18
Bricks 19
Pottery 20
Loom & weaving 21
Knitting 23
Wheel 24
Silk 25
Cement 26
Glass 27
Paper 29
Spectacles 30
Test Your Memory 31
Index 32

Introduction

A long and gradual history of inventions and discoveries has made progress possible in our everyday lives. The existence of scientific inventions dates back to the origin of the modern human race. The prehistoric and middle age inventions played an important role in the evolution of human society. Though these inventions appear small in the present day world, but they completely changed the look of the society of those times. This book highlights a few such inventions which are considered essential to human needs and which have completely changed the outlook of the society.

ANCIENT INVENTIONS

Making fire

At some unknown time, before the beginning of settled life in the Neolithic Revolution, humans learned how to make fire. No doubt the discovery happened at many different times in many different places over a very long period. The knowledge of how to create a spark and to nurture it until it developed into a flame is an intrinsic skill of human society.

Almost without any exception, Stone Age tribes, surviving into modern times, invented the methods of making fire.

> The first simple languages spoken by Homo erectus perhaps developed around 500,000 years ago.

The most common way of making fire was by friction, using a fire drill. This consisted of a stick of hard wood, pointed at one end and a slab of softer wood with a hole in it. If the point was placed in the cavity and rapidly twirled (by rubbing between the palms or by means of a bow string looped round and pulled back and forth), the softer wood began to smoulder. Shreds of dry tinder, placed in the smoldering cavity, could be carefully blown into a flame.

Making fire

Another more sophisticated technique involved was flint and pyrite. Evidence of both methods was found in Neolithic tombs. The useful quality of the naturally occurring mineral pyrite or iron pyrites was that it made a spark if struck with a flint. If the spark was aimed into dry tinder, blowing could achieve a flame.

With the introduction of iron, it was discovered that the same principle applied between flint and steel. This eventually became the standard method of making fire.

The European tinderbox of the 16th century was a portable fire-making kit, consisting of flint, steel, tinder to catch the spark and a match (like the wick of a lamp) to hold the fire in a steady and lasting glow. Not until the 19th century was this equipment replaced by matches in the modern sense.

People have been using fire to cook their food for almost as long as there have been people on Earth. African people invented on-purpose cooking fires probably about one million years ago.

ANCIENT INVENTIONS

In the beginning, people, in Africa, cooked food on outside wood fires. When they left Africa about 60,000 years ago, they brought the idea of cooking food on fires with them all over the world.

Perhaps the last Ice Age, which ended about 10,000 BC, made people invent the idea of lighting fires inside to keep their caves warm.

But by the Late Stone Age, around 6000 BC, people were beginning to live in houses and the houses were in small villages. They needed to be more careful with their wood supply to make it last. They started to use ovens. Also, they began to make burnt pottery around this time, which needed very hot and long fires in a kiln (a sort of oven).

By 4000 BC they started to cook on charcoal fires instead of just using wood. Charcoal is made by slowly burning wood in a kiln with very little air. It burns more efficiently and is hotter than wood.

Making fire

Around 3000 BC, people in West Asia began to use charcoal to smelt copper and tin together into bronze. A hot charcoal fire was needed to smelt metal as fires made out of wood don't burn hot enough.

Blacksmiths needed even hotter fires to smelt iron. The method was not invented until about 1500 BC, by the Hittites in West Asia, and then it spread to the rest of Asia and to Europe from there. African blacksmiths may have invented iron smelting for themselves, about 300 AD.

The Romans, beginning around 200 BC during the Roman Republic, used charcoal fires to heat air and water and piped it through their houses to heat their houses and to get hot water for public and private bath. But most people used small charcoal fires in clay braziers to heat their houses and to cook at home.

In the middle ages in Europe, these pipes went out of use, and people went back to wood or charcoal fires on hearths in their houses. They did start to use chimneys to get the smoke out of their houses.

ANCIENT INVENTIONS

Pigments

Naturally occurring pigments such as ochres and iron oxides have been used as colorants since prehistoric times. Archaeologists have uncovered evidence that early humans used paint for artistic purposes such as body decoration. Pigments and paint grinding equipment are believed to be between 350,000 and 400,000 years old. They existed in a cave at Twin Rivers, near Lusaka, Zambia. Before the Industrial Revolution, the range of colour available for art and decorative uses was technically limited. Most of the pigments in use were earth and mineral pigments or pigments of biological origin. Pigments from unusual sources such as botanical materials, animal waste, insects and molluscs were harvested and traded over long distances. Some colours were costly or impossible to mix with the range of pigments that were available. Blue and purple came to be associated with royalty because of their expense.

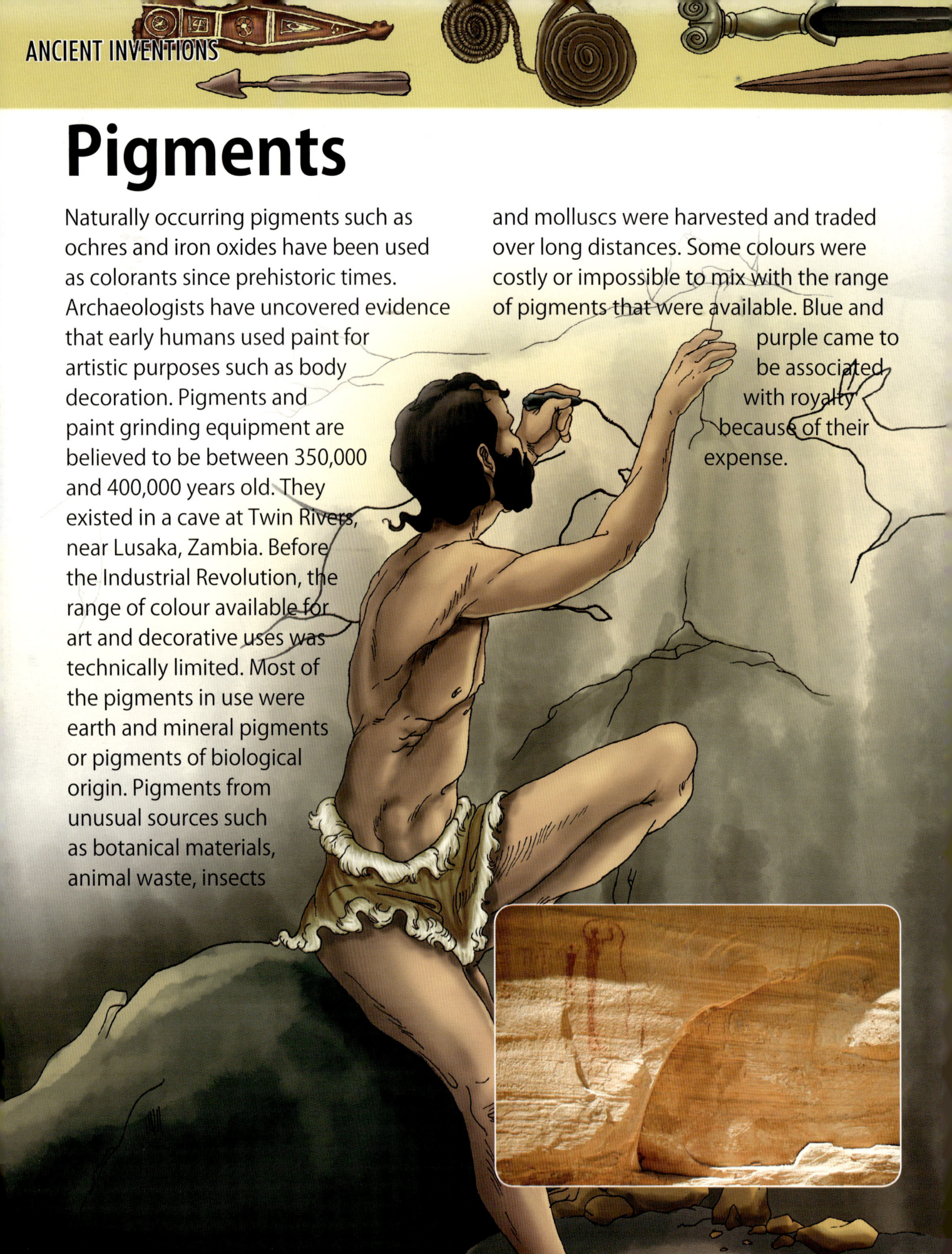

Needle and thread

The needle was probably discovered about 15000 to 20000 years ago. Stone Age people in colder regions of the world used to stitch dried animal skins with leather thongs to get warm clothing. For stitching, they had to make holes in skins and then tie them together with threads.
To speed up the process, bone needle with an eye was developed in the Palaeolithic period. This invention made the process continuous and the same needle created holes and pulled the thread through to stitch the skin. This was one of the major inventions for mankind. The remains of bone or ivory needles were found in ancient European caves and were expected to be more than 15000 years old. The use of bone needles spans a long period, from prehistoric to middle age. The main reasons are that these needles were easy to make and didn't rust. With the invention of metal processing units, bone needles were replaced by smaller and thinner metal needles.

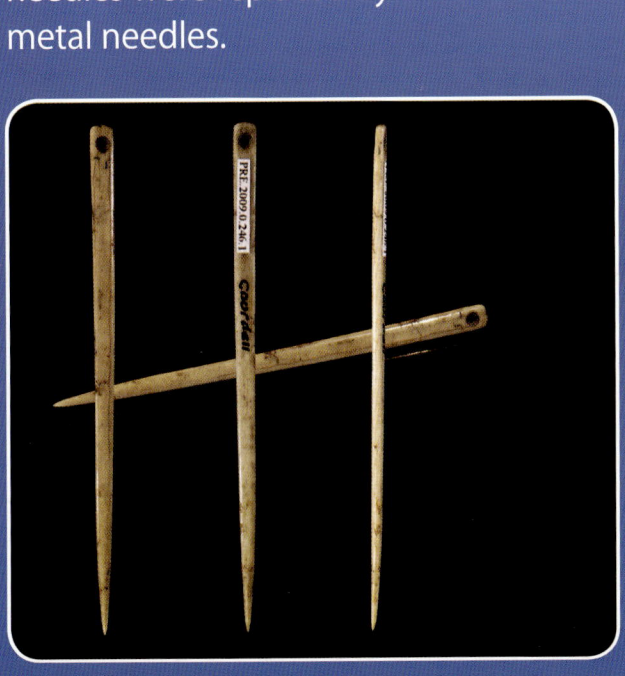

ANCIENT INVENTIONS

The bow and arrow

The bow was made up of a strip of flexible material, most probably wood with a cord linking the ends of strip and the arrow was a straight shaft with a sharp point on one end. The stretching of bow cord created tensile force which moved the arrow.

The first stone arrowheads were discovered in Africa before 25000 BC, which indicates that the bow and arrow most likely developed there as early as 40000 BC. The spear would have come before the bow and both instruments were used side by side. Fire-hardened arrow points, flint tipped arrows, and feathered arrow shafts probably appeared anywhere from 25000 to 18000 BC.

The use of the bow and arrow for hunting and for war dates back to the Paleolithic period in Africa, Asia and Europe. It was widely used in ancient Egypt, Mesopotamia, Persia, the Americas and Europe until the introduction of gunpowder. Arrowheads were first made of burnt wood, then stone or bone, and then metals. Various woods and bones were used for the bow itself.

Cro-Magnon man invented weapons for long distances such as bow and arrows and spear throwers. Their invention of axes allowed them to chop down trees.

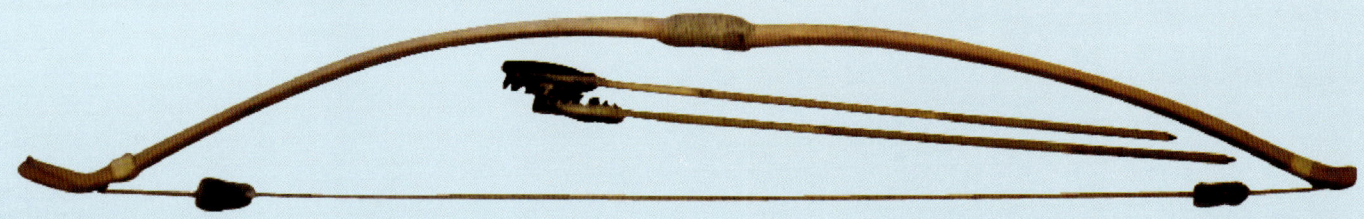

10

The bow and arrow

The bow seems to have been invented by the late Paleolithic or early Mesolithic. The oldest indication for archery in Europe comes from the Stellmoor in the Ahrensburg valley north of Hamburg, Germany and dates from the late Paleolithic about 9000-8000 BC. The arrows were made of pine and consisted of a main-shaft and a 15-20 cm long fore-shaft with a flint point. There are no known definite earlier bows, but stone points which have been identified as arrowheads were made in Africa by about 200,000 years ago.

The oldest bows known so far come from the Holmegaard swamp in Denmark. In the 1940s, two bows were found there. The Holmegaard bows were made of elm and had flat arms and a D-shaped midsection. The centre section was biconvex. The complete bow was 1.50 m long. Bows of Holmegaard-type were in use until the Bronze Age.

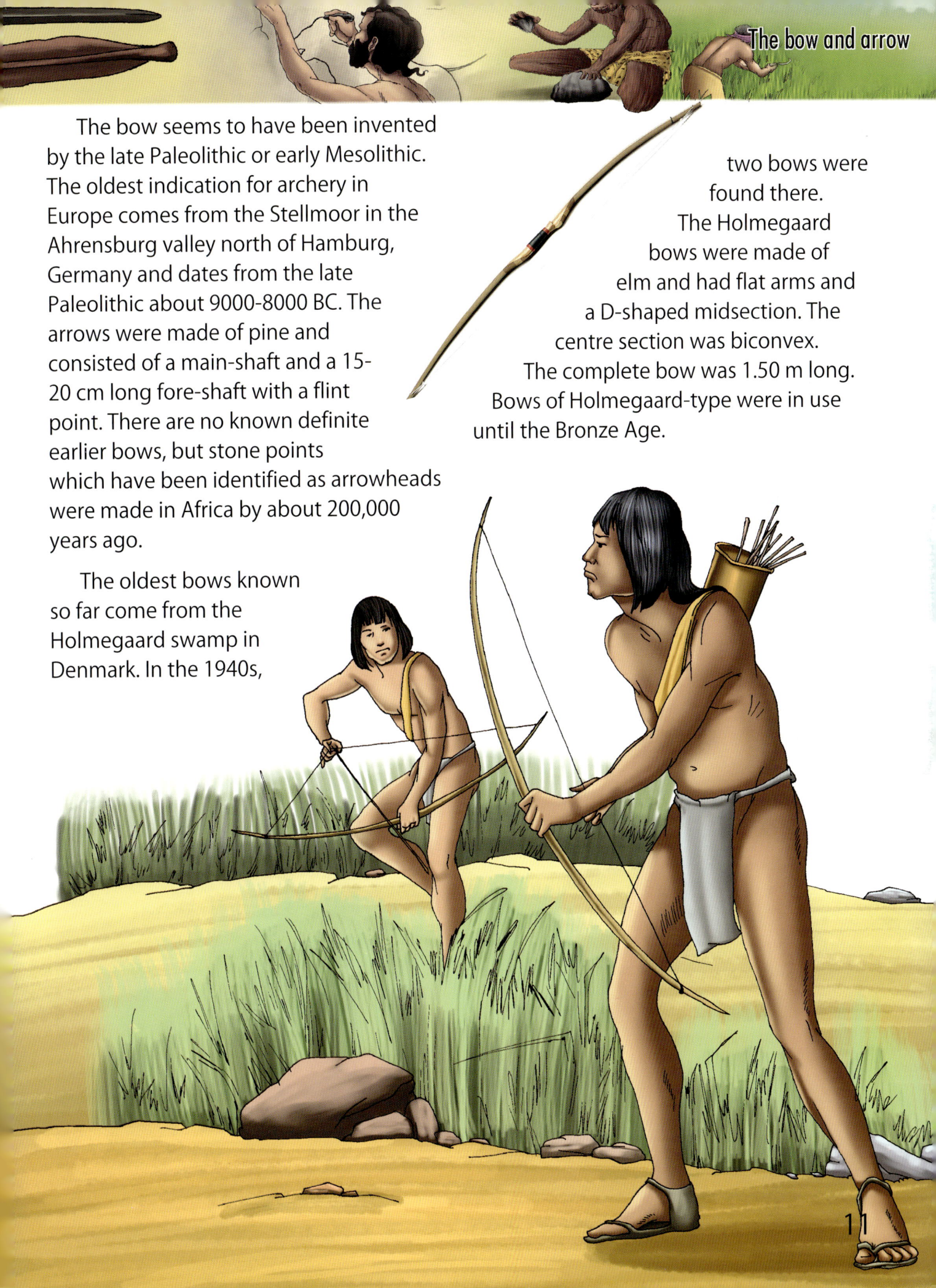

ANCIENT INVENTIONS

Musical instruments

The first known music instruments were flutes. The flute appeared in different forms and locations around the world. A three-hole flute made from a mammoth tusk, (from the Geißenklösterle cave in the German Swabian Alb and dated to 30,000 to 37,000 years ago), and two flutes made from swans' bones excavated a decade earlier (from the same cave in Germany, dated to circa 36,000 years ago) are among the oldest known musical instruments. The flute has been dated to prehistoric times. A fragment of the femur of a juvenile cave bear, with two to four holes, found at Divje Babe in Slovenia and dated to about 43,100 years ago, may also be an early flute. Some early flutes were made out of tibias (shin bones). Playable 9000-year-old Gudi (literally, 'bone flute'), made from the wing bones of red-crowned cranes, with five to eight holes each were excavated from a tomb in Jiahu in the Central Chinese province of Henan.

The boat

Archaeological evidence indicates that humans arrived on New Guinea at least 60,000 years ago, probably by sea from Southeast Asia during an ice age period when the sea was lower and distances between islands shorter. The ancestors of Australian Aborigines and New Guineans went across the Lombok Strait to Sahul by boat over 50,000 years ago.

Evidences from ancient Egypt show that the early Egyptians already knew how to assemble planks of wood into a watertight hull, using tree nails to fasten them together. The 'Khufu ship', a 43.6 m long vessel sealed into a pit in the Giza pyramid complex at the foot of the Great Pyramid of Giza in the Fourth Dynasty around 2,500 BC, is a full-size surviving example which may have fulfilled the symbolic function of a solar barque (a mythological representation of the sun riding in a boat).

13

Clothing

Clothing is one of the major features of all modern societies in the world. Some societies are very strict about the way in which men, women and children should dress, or how different social classes and groups should present themselves. It reflects our notions of grace and beauty. Moreover, it defines the identity and social status of people.

Scientists are still debating when people started wearing clothes but researchers using genetic methods estimated that clothing had been originated around 540,000 years ago.

According to archaeologists and anthropologists, the earliest clothing probably consisted of fur, leather, leaves or grass, draped, wrapped or tied about the body for protection from the weather. Knowledge of such clothing remains probable, since clothing materials got destroyed quickly compared to stone, bone, shell and metal artifacts.

Animal domestication

Between 13,000 and 2,500 B.C., humans domesticated dogs, cats, cattle, goats, horses and sheep from their wild counterparts. Although, the terms 'taming' and 'domestication' are often used interchangeably, they are not the same. Individual wild animals can be tamed to behave in a docile manner around humans. By contrast, domestication is a process that takes place with an entire animal species over many generations.

The dog is thought to have been the first animal to be domesticated by humans, sometime around 13,000–10,000 B.C., from its wolf-like ancestor Canis lupus. Scientists believe that humans adopted cubs and raised them. They do not deny the possibility that humans might have accepted, in their group, the entry of some of the less fierce wolves that hung around their camps scrounging for leftover food. In either event, humans soon found dogs to be a welcome addition. The arrangement benefited both sides, as domesticated wolves helped humans with hunting and guarding duties and shared the food that was obtained.

ANCIENT INVENTIONS

The ancient Egyptians are usually credited with domesticating wild cats around 4,000 B.C. The Egyptians most likely raised cats from small kittens to protect their grain stores from rats and mice. Cat domestication is strongly associated with the establishment of permanent settlements and the growing and storage of grains. Cats became important to agricultural societies, just as dogs had been important to hunting cultures.

The domestication of livestock—chiefly pigs, cows, sheep, horses and goats is thought to have occurred between 9,000 and 5,000 B.C. as agriculture became more of a factor in human societies scattered across Asia and Europe. Scientists can estimate these dates based on evidence from excavated archaeological sites.

Chickens were domesticated from Asian jungle fowl around 3,500 B.C. as a source of meat and eggs. Camels were domesticated around 2,500 B.C. Other early domesticated animals were turkeys and musk ducks in Central America, llamas, guinea pigs, and alpacas in South America.

Ropes

The use of ropes for hunting, pulling, fastening, attaching, carrying, lifting and climbing dates back to prehistoric times and has always been essential to mankind's technological progress. It is likely that the earliest 'ropes' were naturally occurring lengths of plant fibre, such as vines, which were soon followed by the first attempts at twisting and braiding these strands together to form the first proper ropes. Fossilised fragments of 'probably two-ply laid rope of about 7 mm diameter' were found in Lascaux cave, dating to approximately 15,000 BC. The ancient Egyptians were probably the first civilization to develop special tools to make ropes. Egyptian rope dates back to 4000 to 3500 B.C. and was generally made of water reed fibres. Other ropes in ancient times were made from the fibres of date palms, flax, grass, papyrus, leather, or animal hair.

> **The ancient Egyptians were probably the first to develop special tools to make rope. Egyptian rope dates back to 4000 to 3500 B.C. and was generally made of water reed fibres.**

17

ANCIENT INVENTIONS

Agriculture

The practice of agriculture first began around 8000 BC in the Fertile Crescent of Mesopotamia (part of present day Iraq, Turkey, Syria and Jordan which was then greener). This region was home to the greatest diversity of annual plants and according to one study 32 of the 56 largest grass seeds.

The first crops to be cultivated were all crops of edible seeds, wheat, barley, peas, lentils, chickpeas, bitter vetch and flax. These plants were all readily storable and grew quickly. They had to undergo a few genetic changes to be of use to farmers. In several other regions worldwide local crop domestication took place independently.

In China, rice and millet were cultivated by 7500 BC, followed by the beans mung, soy and aduki. In the Sahel region of Africa, local rice and sorghum were cultivated by 5000 BC. Local crops were cultivated independently in West Africa and possibly in New Guinea and Ethiopia. Three regions of the Americas independently grew corn, squashes, potato and sunflowers.

Prehistoric men built villages along rivers or wherever the ground was fertile enough for crops to grow. Archaeologists have found out that some villages that are believed to have been built more than 8,000 years ago. Ancient villages, such as Jericho, survive to this day!

Bricks

An important innovation in the Neolithic period was the use of bricks. In their simplest form (still familiar today in many hot regions), bricks were shaped by pressing mud or clay into a mould. The damp blocks were then left to bake hard in the sun. Bricks of this kind were known in Jericho from about 8000 BC.

The Mesolithic period of the Stone Age saw the birth of tools like fishing tackle, stone adzes and wooden objects like canoes and bows which have been found at some sites.

The more durable type of brick, baked in a kiln was an offshoot of the potter's technology. Kiln bricks were widely used in the two earliest civilizations, Mesopotamia and Egypt, often to provide the outer surface of walls on an inner core of sun-dried brick.

Pottery

One of the most useful of all human discoveries is pottery. Indeed, a standard distinction made by archaeologists, when describing successive cultures in an area, was between groups which are 'aceramic' (without pottery) and others which had mastered the technology of clay and kiln.

In western Asia, where the Neolithic Revolution was the most advanced, the first pottery at sites such as Catal Huyuk dated from about 6500 BC.

The earliest wares at Catal Huyuk were made by one of the standard methods of primitive potters. Rings or coils of clay were built up from a circular base. The walls of the pot were then smoothed and thinned (by simultaneous pressure on the inner and outer surfaces) before being fired in a bread oven or in the most elementary of kilns— a hole in the ground, above which a bonfire was lit.

Early Neolithic pottery was usually undecorated. Where there was decoration, it took the form of patterns cut or pressed into the damp clay.

Loom & weaving

Weaving of cloth required a loom—a structure which will hold taut the vertical threads (the warp), while the weaver snaked each horizontal thread in and out to form the weft. When the threads of the weft were pressed down tight to form a solid mesh with the warp, a section of the cloth at the bottom of the loom was complete. A pattern was achieved by varying the colour of the threads in the warp and the weft.

The earliest known evidence of a loom comes from Egypt in about 4400 BC, but some method of supporting the warp exists from the beginning of weaving. The threads must either be suspended (held taut by a weight at the bottom) or else must be stretched in the rigid frame of a conventional loom.

A number of archeologists believe that Middle Paleolithic societies may have practiced the earliest form of totemism or animal worship.

ANCIENT INVENTIONS

Until recently the earliest known scraps of cloth were woven from wool. Dating from about 5800 BC, they come from Catal Huyuk in Anatolia. Similarly, the first known example of linen had been from about 5000 BC in Egypt where flax (an indigenous wild plant in the Mediterranean region) was cultivated. But a small woven fragment discovered in 1993 near the upper reaches of the Tigris probably pushed back the available evidence. It appeared to be linen and had been dated to about 7000 BC.

Cotton was grown in both Eurasia and America; woven cotton survived from about 2500 BC in the Indus valley and slightly later in Peru. The most precisely localized source of any major fabric is China, where pieces of woven silk were known from about 2850 BC.

Knitting

Knitting as a concept, was very simple but extremely hard to imagine. It was likely, therefore, to be one of the few technological developments in ancient history to have an actual inventor.

Knitting first appeared in the Roman Empire, in the 3rd century AD. The earliest examples to survive were socks found in the tombs of Egypt. Until this time the feet had usually been kept warm and protected within the shoe by wrapping them in strips of cloth or leather. In the 2nd century AD the Romans invented a tailored sock, made of pieces of cloth sewn together. But these lacked the elasticity of a knitted fabric. Eventually the demand for knitted stockings was so great that the first knitting, devised in 1589 was an early landmark of the Industrial Revolution.

According to archaeologists and anthropologists, the earliest clothing probably were made of fur, leather, leaves or grass, wrapped or tied about the body for protection.

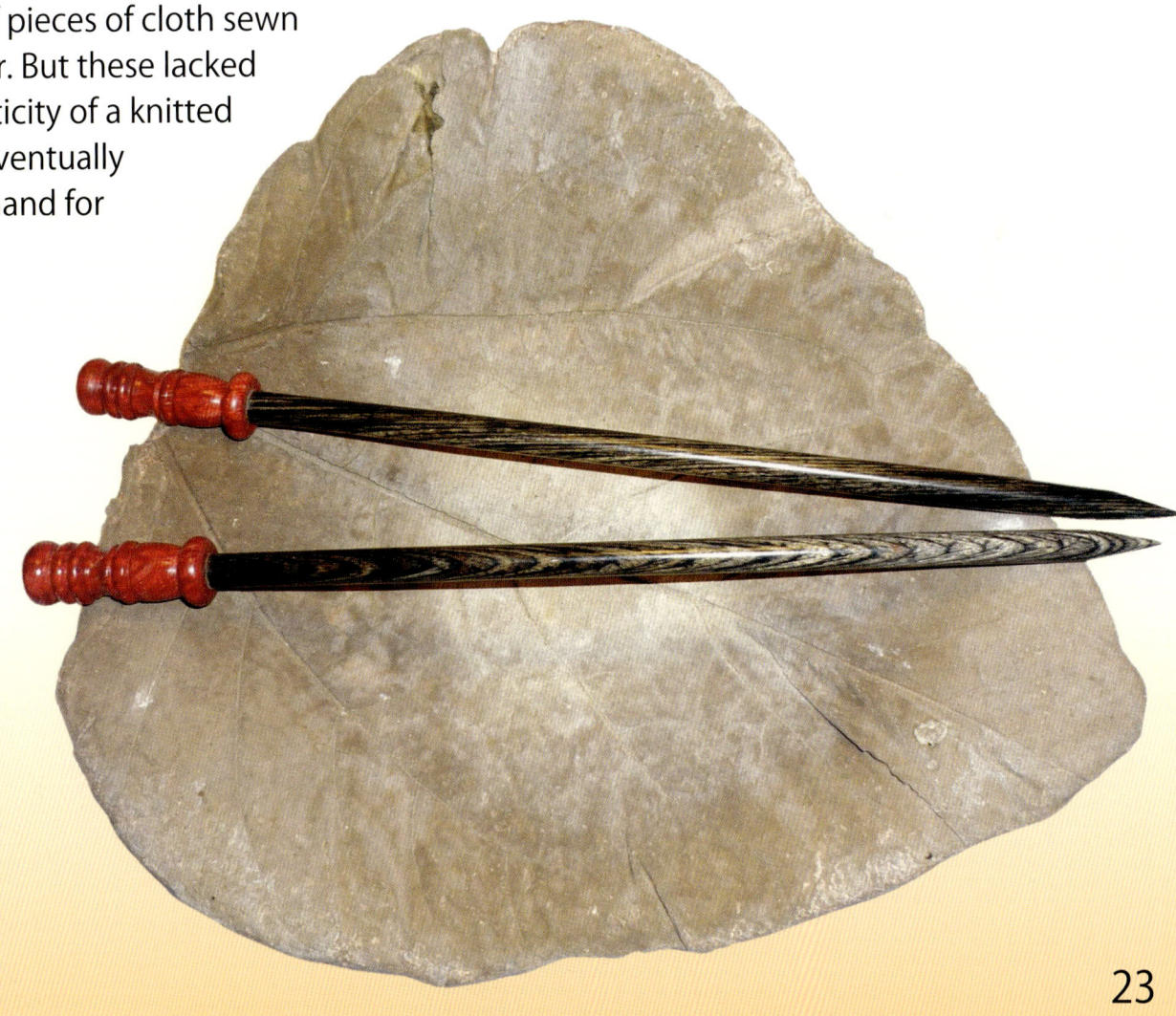

ANCIENT INVENTIONS

Wheel

Up till now, it is still a mystery as to who invented the wheel and when the wheel was invented. According to archaeologists, it was probably invented in around 8,000 B.C. in Asia. The oldest wheel known however, was discovered in Mesopotamia and probably dates back to 3,500 B.C. This wheel was believed to have been made by the Sumerians. It was made of planks of wood joined together.

The wheel was furthered improved on later by the Egyptians, who made wheels with spokes, which could be found on Egyptian chariots of around 2000 BC. In Ancient India, chariots with spoked wheels dating back to around 1500 B.C. were also discovered. The Greeks too, adopted the idea of wheel-making from the Egyptians and made further improvements to it. Later, during the time of the Roman Empire, the Romans too engaged themselves in wheel-making and produced the greatest variety of wheeled vehicles. They had chariots for war, hunting and racing, two-wheeled farm carts, covered carriages, heavy four-wheeled freight wagons and passenger coaches.

Silk

It is believed that the Chinese first started making silk around 2,700 BC. Legend has it that Empress Si Ling Chi discovered silk when a silkworm moth cocoon fell from a mulberry tree into her tea. After some experiment, she finally managed to weave the silk filament into a piece of fabric.

The process of making silk weaving is still the same today. Known as **sericulture**, the cocoons are placed in hot water to release the silk filaments and kill the silkworm larvae. The filaments are combined to form yarn, wound and finally dried. Each cocoon can yield around 500 to 1,200 yards of silk!

Silk was considered China's most valuable trade commodity, resulting in the famous Silk Road trading route. Silk making was a closely-guarded government secret until AD 300 when it was leaked out to India.

ANCIENT INVENTIONS

Cement

Builders in Greek cities on the coast of Turkey invented cement in about 200 BC as a structural material, in place of weaker mortars such as gypsum plaster (used in Egypt) or bitumen (in Mesopotamia). The secret of the new material was the lime which held together sand, water and clay.

The Romans subsequently used finely ground volcanic lava in place of clay, deriving it mainly from the region of Pozzuoli. Their cement, known for this reason as pozzolanic was the strongest mortar in history until the development of Portland cement. When small fragments of volcanic rubble were included, the result was concrete. It made possible the great arches and aqueducts of Roman architecture and played its part in the construction of the Roman roads.

Glass

In Phoenicia, in about 1500 BC, the making of glass became a practical craft. Glass beads were known in Egypt 1000 years earlier. They were shaped and formed accidentally when the necessary materials that make glass mixed in the heat. The composition of glass was unknown at that time.

The Phoenicians discovered how to make glass on a predictable basis (from sand, limestone and sodium carbonate) and they invented ways of shaping this difficult but magically appealing substance into small vessels. The basic method, known as core-forming, consisted of applying the molten glass to the outside of a solid core of soft clay. When the glass cooled and hardened, the core could be scraped out.

Natural pigments such as ochres and iron oxides have been used as colorants since prehistoric times.

ANCIENT INVENTIONS

These Phoenician skills were carried south to Egypt during the 15th century BC after the shores of the eastern Mediterranean were conquered by the Egyptian pharaoh, Thutmose. Small bottles, to hold precious oils for cosmetic purposes, became treasured items in rich Egyptian households. The body of the vessel was usually a transparent blue, sometimes decorated with thread-like rings of white, yellow or green applied to the surface.

Glass was an expensive rarity, and remained so in Egypt and elsewhere (Mesopotamia, Greece, Persia) until Roman times. The oldest fragments of

glass vases date back to the 16th century BC and were found in Mesopotamia. Hollow glass production was also evolving around this time in Egypt, and there was evidence of other ancient glassmaking activities emerging independently in Mycenae (Greece), China and North Tyrol.

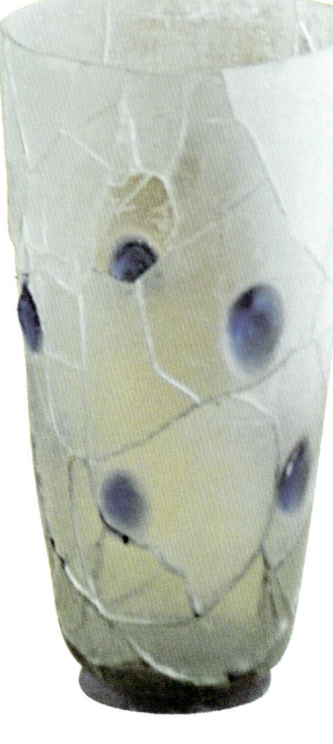

28

Paper

Paper was invented in China some 3,000 years after the ancient Egyptians used papyrus for writing. Cai Lun, a government official from the eastern Han dynasty made paper by mixing the bark of a mulberry tree and bamboo fibres with water, draining and drying the mixture on a flat bamboo frame.

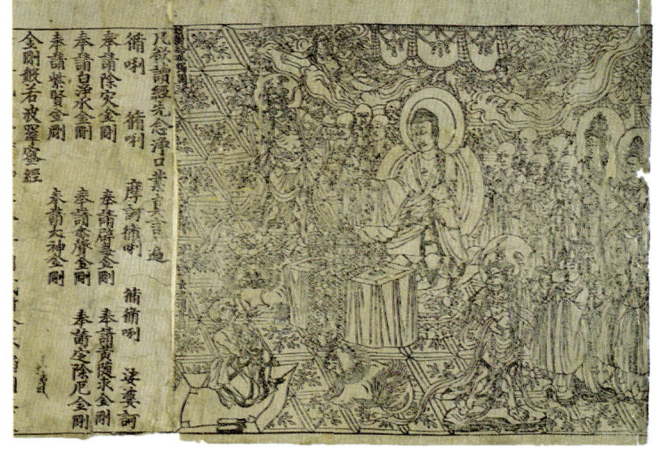

During the Tang and Song dynasties, papers were developed for different purposes. They included hemp paper, hide paper, bamboo paper and xuan paper made from a kind of pine tree used particularly for calligraphy.

Progress in papermaking was complemented by the development of printing. Block printing, or xylography, was used in China by the 7th century and the earliest known printed text, a Buddhist scripture was printed in AD 868.

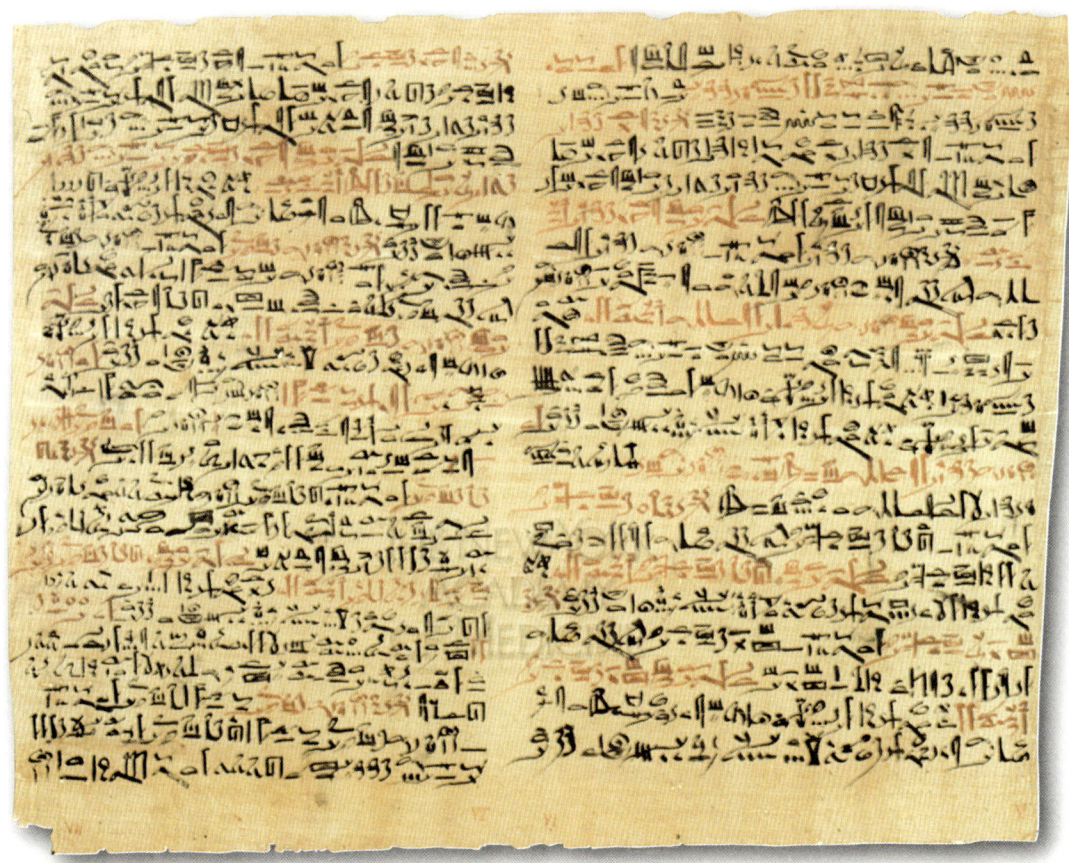

ANCIENT INVENTIONS

Spectacles

During the 13th century it was discovered that a crystal with a curved surface could help the elderly to read. Mounted in a holder, such a lens was simply a small magnifying glass. The philosopher-scientist Roger Bacon referred to the use of a lens in a text of 1268. At this time it would be shaped and smoothed from a lump of quartz.

Soon, probably in Florence during the 1280s, the idea evolved of placing two lenses in a frame which could be held in front of the eyes. It was a natural next step to perch this frame on the nose. Spectacles, hinged at the centre to grip the nose, appeared quite frequently in paintings of the 15th century.

As the demand increased, glass replaced quartz as the material for lenses. Early spectacles all used convex lenses to redress long sight (difficulty in seeing things which are close). By the 16th century it was discovered that concave lenses would compensate for short sight (difficulty in seeing distant objects). And so, the two regular forms of spectacles had been created.

The Egyptians invented the clock which is so essential to us. They invented two types of clocks— sun clocks and water clocks.

Test Your MEMORY

1. When was the needle discovered?

2. When were the first stone arrowheads discovered?

3. What was the most common way of making a fire?

4. When did people begin to live in houses?

5. When did agriculture first begin?

6. How are bricks shaped?

7. Where does the earliest known evidence of a loom come from?

8. Where do the earliest known silk date back from?

9. Name two naturally occurring pigments.

10. Where did knitting first appear?

11. When was cement first discovered?

12. Where do the oldest fragments of glass vases date back to?

Index

A
anthropologists 14
archaeologists 8, 14, 18, 20, 24
archery 11
arrow 10, 11
arrow shafts 10

B
block printing 29
bone needle 9
bow cord 10
Bronze Age 11

C
chariots 24
clothing 9, 14
concave lenses 30
convex lenses 30

D
discoveries 3, 20

E
evolution 3

F
flutes 12

G
glass 27, 28, 30
gunpowder 10

I
inventions 3, 9
iron oxides 8

K
Khufu ship 13
kiln 6, 19, 20

M
Mesolithic 11, 19
Mesopotamia 10, 18, 19, 24, 26, 28
middle age 3, 9
mulberry tree 25, 29

N
needle 9

O
ochres 8

P
Palaeolithic period 9
paper 29
pigments 8

Pre
prehistoric 3, 8, 9, 12, 15, 17, 18

Q
quartz 30

R
ropes 17

S
silk 22, 25
silkworm moth cocoon 25
solar barque 13
spear 10, 11
spokes 24
Stone Age 4, 6, 9, 19
stone arrowheads 10

T
tensile force 10

W
wheel 24

X
xylography 29

Z
Zambia 8

* Maps not to scale; for illustration purpose only.

PEGASUS ENCYCLOPEDIA LIBRARY

DISCOVERIES AND INVENTIONS
COMPUTERS

Edited by: Anil Kumar Tomar, Pallabi B. Tomar
Managing editor: Tapasi De
Designed by: Vijesh Chahal, Anil Kumar, Rohit Kumar
Illustrated by: Suman S. Roy, Tanoy Choudhury
Colouring done by: Vinay Kumar, Sonu, Kiran Kumari & Pradeep Kumar

COMPUTERS

CONTENTS

What is a computer? 3

Characteristics of a computer 4

Brief history of computers 5

Types of computers 9

How does a computer work? 12

Test Your Memory 31

Index 32

What is a computer?

The word computer was devised for a computing machine which can perform calculations on large numerical data. It is an electronic device that receives data and a set of instructions, processes the data as per provided instructions and provides output in the form of information. In today's world, computers are an essential part of everyday life and perform a wide range of tasks. They are used everywhere throughout society in the storage and handling of data, from homes to offices, schools and colleges to research centres, secret governmental files to banking transactions.

Printer

Monitor

Processor (computer)

Headphone

Speaker

Keyboard

PC Camera

Mouse

COMPUTERS

Characteristics of a computer

Diligence

A computer is free from monotony, tiredness, lack of concentration etc. It can continuously repeat the same work for number of times without getting bored and can work for long hours without getting tired.

Versatility

A computer is a versatile machine and can perform various tasks of different fields at the same time. The same system can be used for calculations, entertainment, education and many other works.

Accuracy

A computer always provides an accurate result. Errors can occur, but these are mainly human created due to wrong input of data and instructions. Computers do not have their own brain thus generally regarded as 'GIGO' that means garbage in garbage out.

Astonishing fact

Sweden is the country with the highest percentage of Internet users (75 per cent).

Brief history of computers

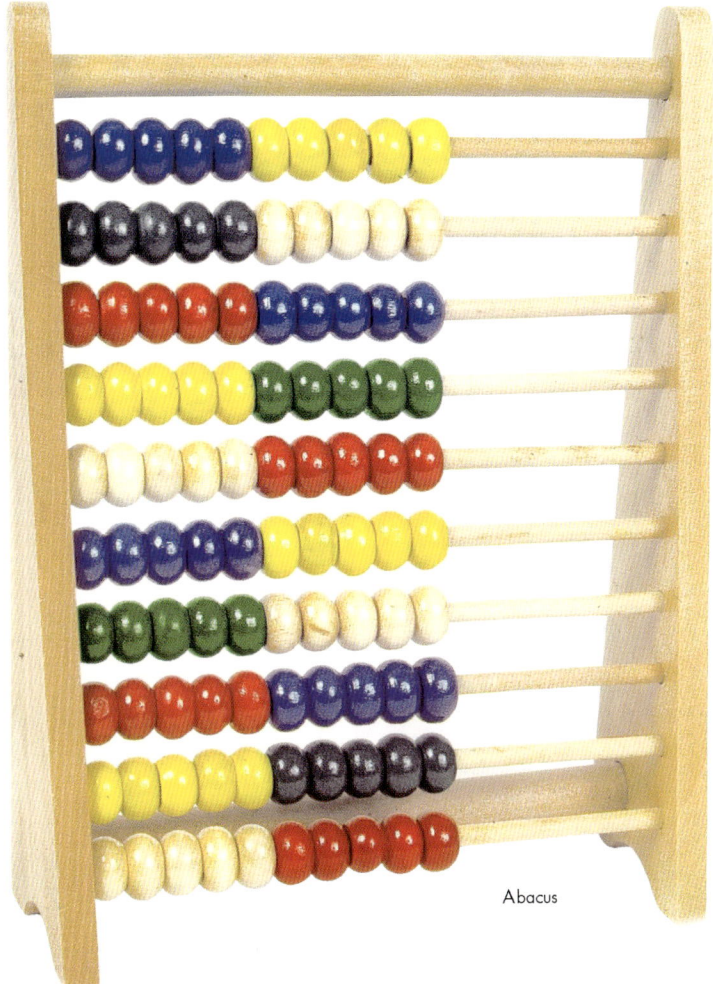
Abacus

Ancient Times: Abacus is the earliest known device used for computations. It dates back to ancient times and was invented by the Chinese. Ten beads strung onto wires attached to a frame were devised for addition and subtraction of small numbers. This device is still used in play schools to teach kids.

17th Century: John Napier devised a system, known as Napier's bones where he put the logarithms on a set of ivory rods. By sliding the numbers up and down, he invented a very primitive slide rule and this marks the beginning of logarithms.

1642: Blaise Pascal developed the first real calculator. This calculator was devised to carry out additions and subtractions by using a series of very light rotating wheels.

Astonishing fact

The command 'Ctrl+Alt+Delete' was written by David Bradley.

Pascal's calculator

COMPUTERS

Jacquard loom

Difference engine

1690: Gottfried van Leibnitz developed a calculating machine that could add, subtract, multiply and divide.

1834: Joseph Jacquard developed punched cards to control the loom patterns. These cards were programmed with instructions and are considered as the ancestor of the IBM punched cards for information storage.

1812: Charles Babbage designed and built the **difference engine**. In 1833, he also designed a machine capable of any type of calculation and called it the **analytic engine**. Babbage is known as the father of the modern day computers.

Brief history of computers

1890: Dr Herman Hollerith invented a punched card device to analyze the US census data. This machine was called **Tabulating Machine**. He set up the Tabulating Machine Company which manufactured and marketed punched cards. In 1911, he merged his company with other companies to form the International Business Machine Corporation (IBM).

1944: Howard Aiken devised the first automatic calculator, Mark I, through collaboration with Harvard University, IBM, and the U.S. War Department.

1945: Jon Von Neumann developed the first stored-program computer, the EDVAC (Electronic Discrete Variable Automatic Computer). This machine marked the beginning of the computer age.

Tabulating Machine

COMPUTERS

The EDVAC was built for the U.S. Army's Ballistics Research Laboratory by the University of Pennsylvania. The computer that was built was to be binary with automatic addition, subtraction, multiplication, programmed division and automatic checking with a memory capacity of 1,000 words. Physically EDVAC had almost 6,000 vacuum tubes and 12,000 diodes. It consumed 56 kw of power. It covered 490 ft^2 of floor and weighed almost 7,850 kg! The typical operating personnel were thirty people for each eight-hour shift.

1946: J. Presper Eckert and John W. Mauchly invented the first electronic computer 'ENIAC' (Electronic Numerical Integrator and Calculator).

Types of computers

Computers are broadly divided into two groups depending on the type of data they process— analog computers and digital computers.

Analog computers

Analog computers do arithmetic and logical operations by processing

> **Astonishing fact**
> One of the world's leading computer and computer peripheral manufacturer Hewlett Packard was first started in a garage at Palo Alto in the year 1939.

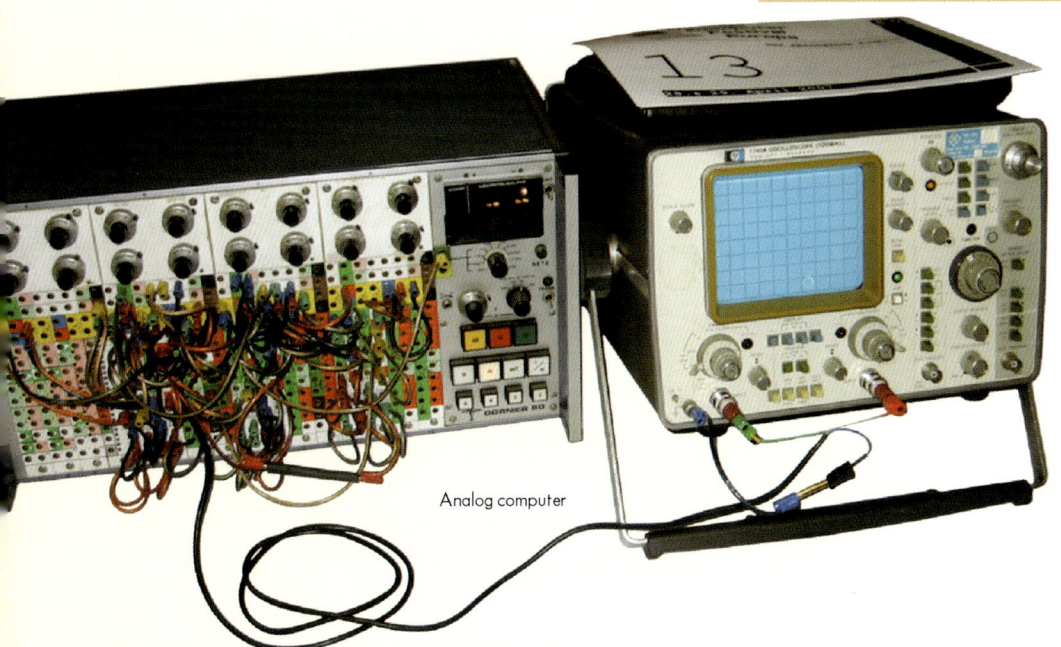
Analog computer

principles of binary mathematics where everything is represented by binary numbers (0 and 1). Most of the modern day computers are digital computers.

continuous physical data such as temperature, pressure, weight, power density or voltage. These computers use analog signals as input and output source. They utilize mechanical, hydraulic or electrical energy for operation. They are only special purpose computers.

Digital computers

Digital computers use digital signals to process the data. They work on the

Digital computer

COMPUTERS

Based on capacity, speed and reliability, computers can be classified into four categories.

Micro computers

These are the most common and abundant computers which are also known as Personal Computers. These are single user machines which have less memory and slow processing speed. These are most popular computers due to their small size and low cost. Personal computers are of many types and some of them are desktops, work stations, notebooks, tablet computers, and handheld computers etc.

Mini computers

Mini computers are small in size and have low processing speed with capabilities between the range of a personal desktop computer and a mainframe. These computers are used in small offices, government departments and educational institutes where small networking is required to connect several terminals. These computers are commonly used as network servers. Single user mini computers are also used for some specific tasks by researchers, designers, engineers etc.

Types of computers

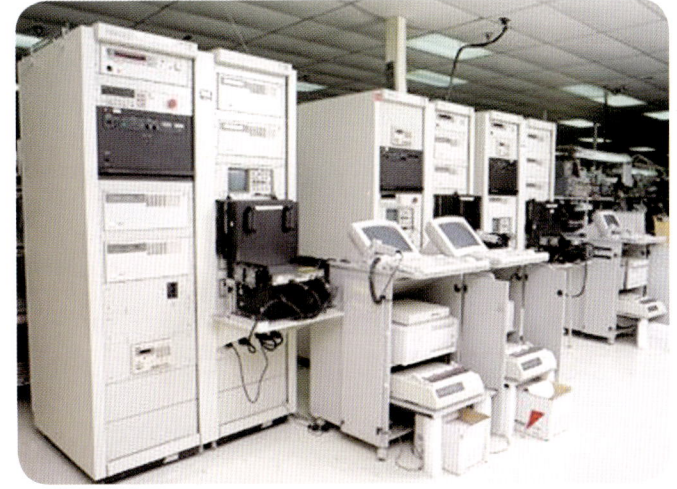

Super computers

A super computer is the most powerful, fastest and most expensive type of computer systems which can perform trillions of calculations per second! It consists of large number of processors connected together for parallel processing. It is used to process large amount of data and to solve the complicated scientific problems. Super computers are mainly used in large organizations, research laboratories, aerospace centres, large industrial units etc. Some of the important purposes are weather forecasting, analysis of nuclear reactions, predicting the interactions of millions of atoms, aircraft designing, automotive design, and online banking etc. Some of the super computers are CRAY series, PARAM and ETA A-10 etc.

Mainframe computers

Mainframes are large and high-performance powerful computer systems to handle the processing of thousands of users at same the time. These computers are large in size, highly expensive and have high processing speed.

COMPUTERS

How does a computer work?

A computer should always consist of input device, central processing unit (CPU), storage device and output device. The data and instructions are given by user through input devices like keyboard. CPU is the brain of computers where all the processing tasks are performed. CPU processes the data step by step according to provided user instructions. The processed data is called information which is visualized by output unit such as Visualizing Display Unit (VDU) which is commonly known as Monitor.

Astonishing fact

The first Apple computer was built by Steve Jobs and Steve Wozniak. It was made by using parts they got for free from their employers!

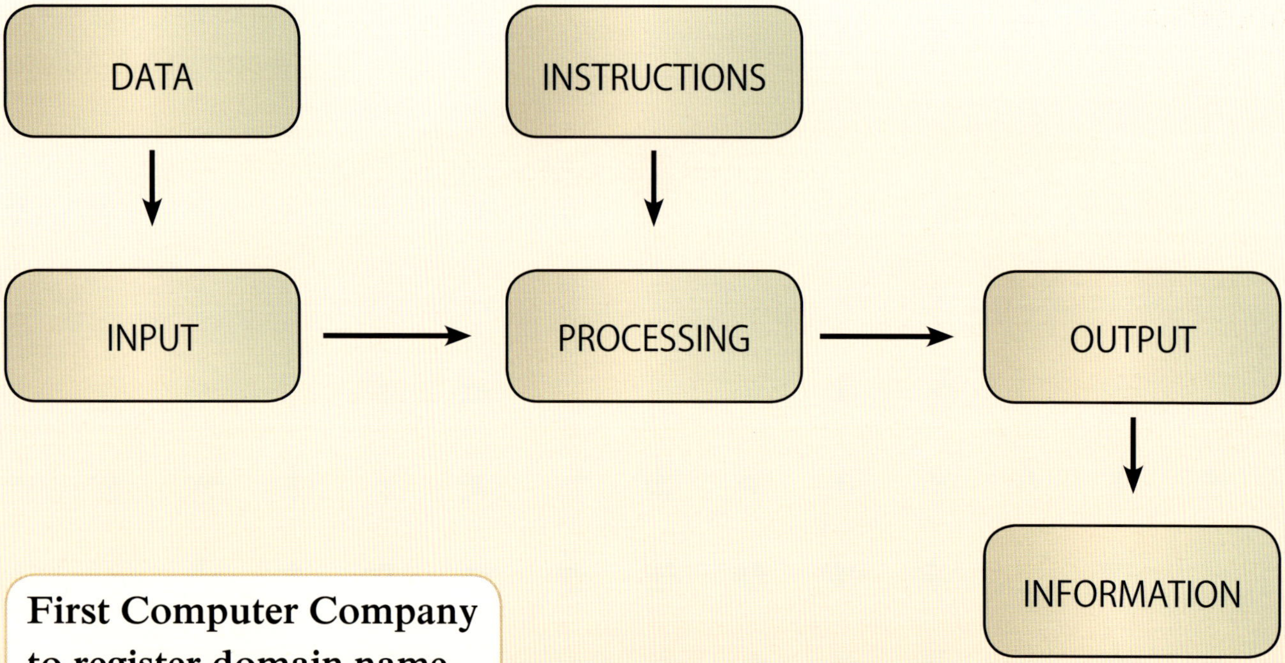

```
DATA                INSTRUCTIONS
  ↓                      ↓
INPUT  →  PROCESSING  →  OUTPUT
                            ↓
                       INFORMATION
```

First Computer Company to register domain name was 'Digital Equipment Corporation'.

Input devices

A computer user enters data, commands and programs into the CPU using input devices. The main function of input devices is to convert human understandable signals into the machine language. Each entry from keyboard is converted into binary codes (a string of 0 and 1). The most common input device is the keyboard. Other important input devices are mouse, light pen, joysticks, scanners, digital camera, optical character recognition (OCR) devices, Magnetic ink character recognition (MICR) devices, touch screens, microphones and many more. The storage devices (CD, DVD, pen drive, hard disk etc.) can also be used to input data.

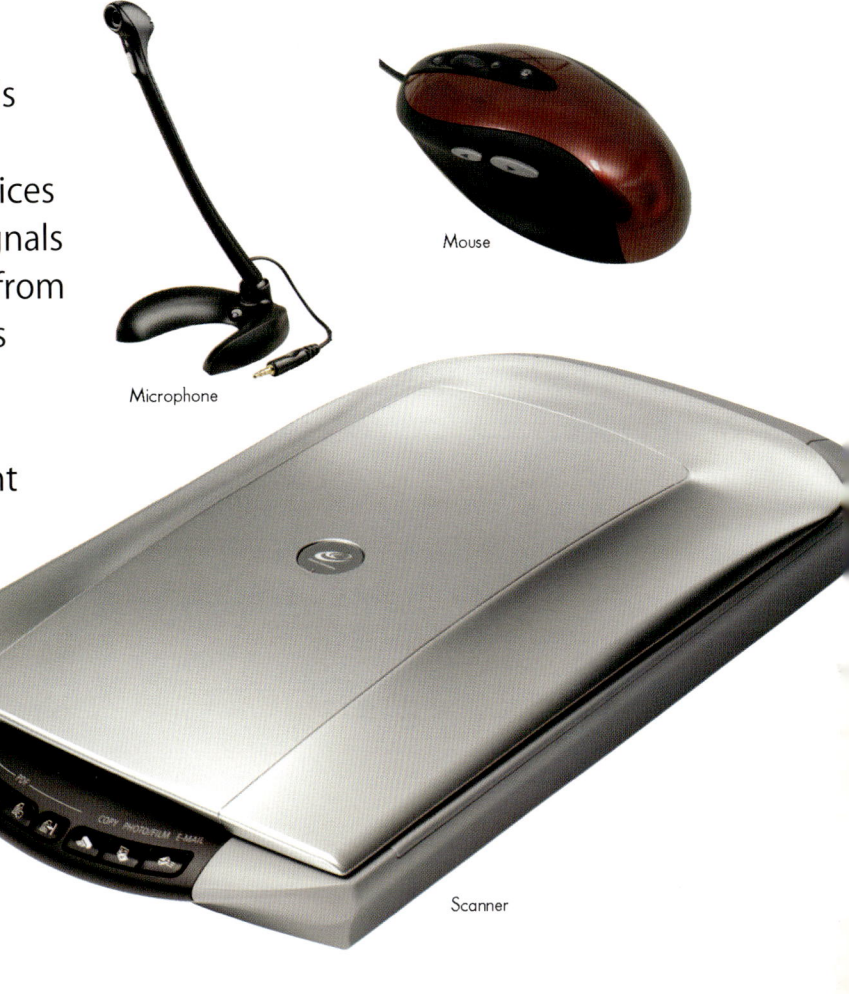

Mouse

Microphone

Scanner

Keyboard

First hard disk drive was introduced by Seagate in 1979, which could hold 5 M.B. of data.

Central Processing Unit

The CPU is the main functional unit of a computer system. It performs arithmetic and logical calculations and also controls the operations of other system elements. All operations are performed by specific integrated circuits (ICs). These circuits are integrated on a chip which is known as a **Microprocessor**. Microprocessors are used in most of today's personal computers.

The CPU consists of three major functional units which are connected through internal buses.

- Memory unit or registers
- Control unit
- Arithmetic/Logic unit

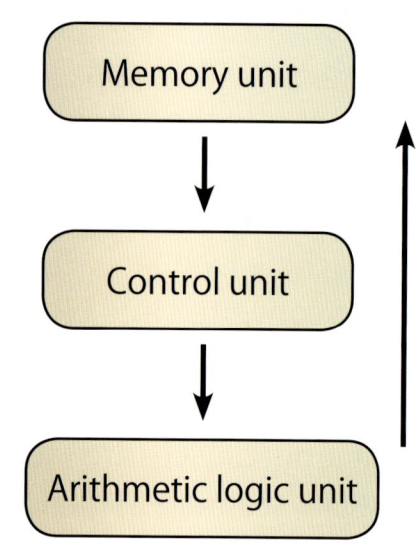

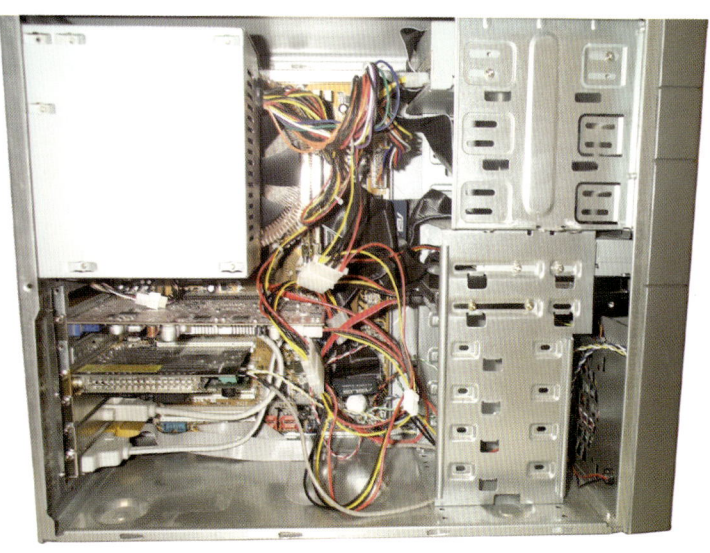

Memory unit/Registers

All the user instructions and input data are temporarily stored in the registers. Thus, registers are also known as temporary storage areas. The major functions of this unit are:

- Registers hold the input data which will be processed.
- Registers also keep the track of user instructions.
- They store intermediate results which are used in the next step of instructions as input.
- They keep the address of storage locations of results.

Control unit

The control unit is one of the most important units for better functioning of a computer system. This unit controls all the operations of a system. The main functions of this unit include:

- This unit distributes CPU time for different operations.
- It regulates execution of all the operations.
- It also reads the patterns of data in a designated register and translates the pattern into an activity.
- This unit decides the order in which all the operations will be performed.

Arithmetic/Logic Unit

The arithmetic/logic unit gives the chip its calculating ability and permits arithmetical and logical operations.

Internal bus

Internal bus is a network of communication wires that connects all the internal units of the CPU with each other and also with the external components of a computer system. These buses are classified as the following:

- Control Bus is used by a CPU for communicating with other devices within the computer.

- Address Bus is a one way connection that handles the location of data in memory addresses.

- Data Bus reads data from memory and writes new data into memory. This is a two way communication line.

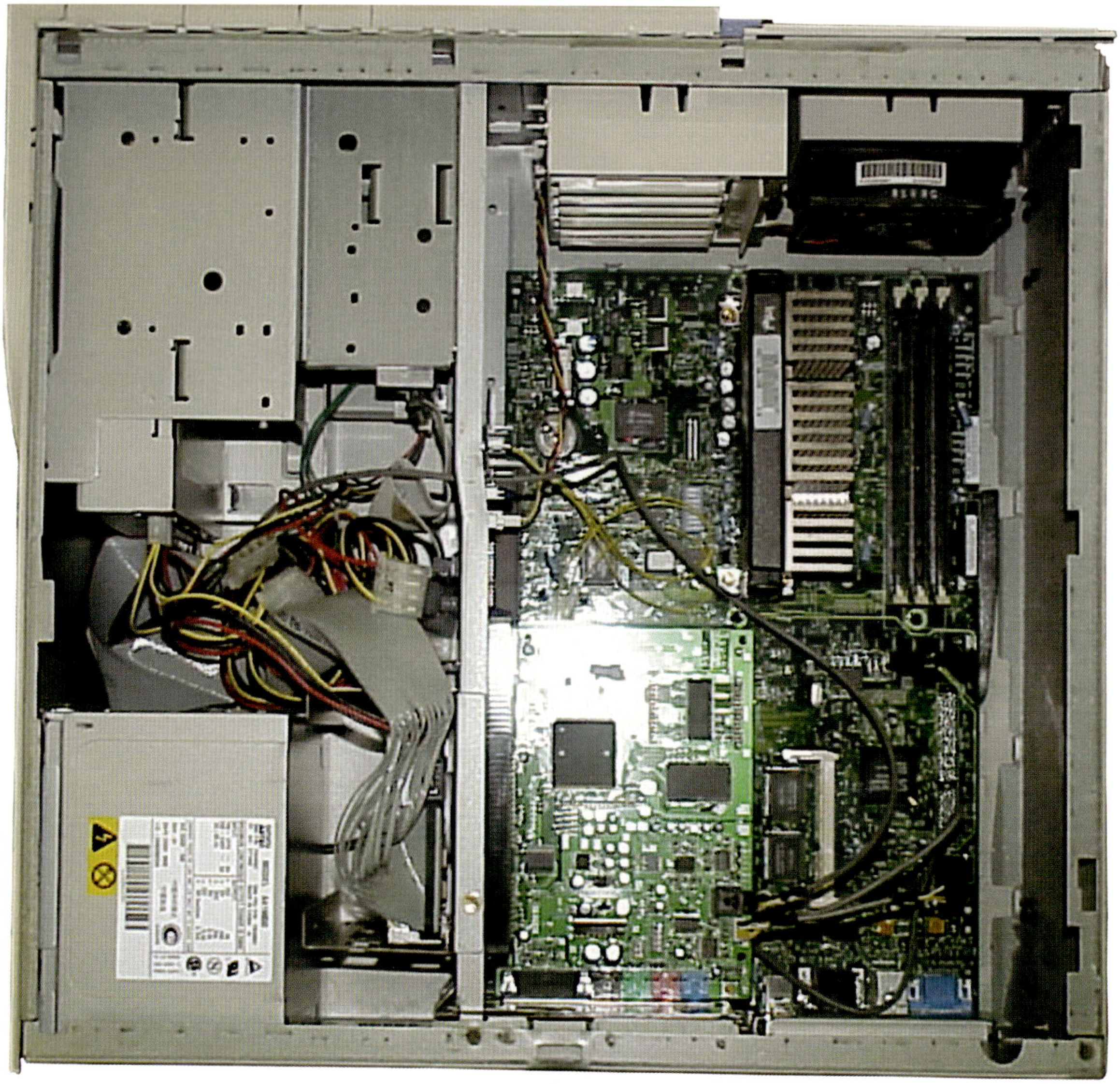

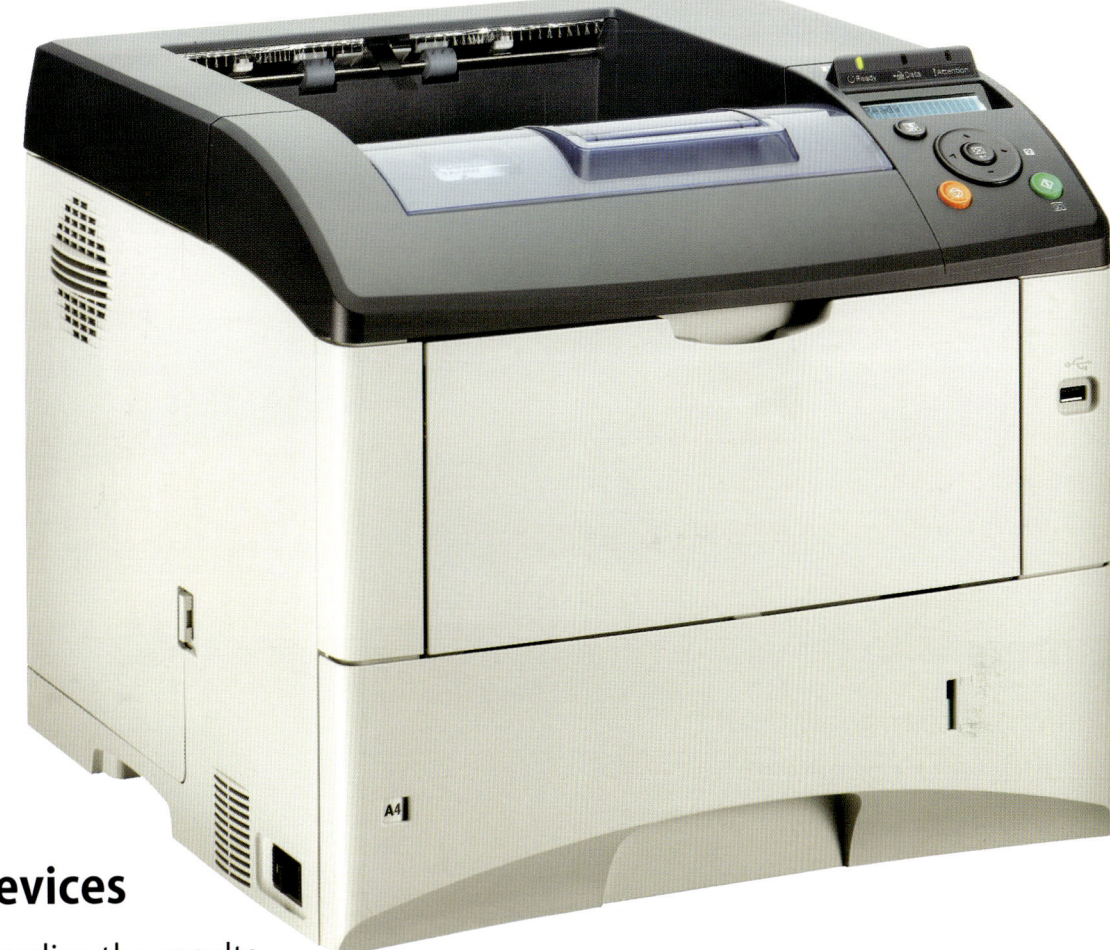

Output devices

A user can visualize the results of data processed by CPU by output devices. The main function of output devices is to convert the results into human understandable form from machine language. The most common output device is Video Display unit (VDU) which is also known as monitor. A monitor displays characters and graphics on a television-like screen. Other output devices are printers, plotters, speakers and secondary storage devices etc.

COMPUTERS

Printers

Printers are commonly used output devices connected to computer system to print text and graphics on the plain papers. There are many types of printers to fulfill the requirements of the specific user. The most commonly used printers are:

- Dot-matrix Printer
- Inkjet Pinter
- Laser Printer

Dot-matrix printers create characters by striking pins against an ink ribbon. Each pin makes a dot and combinations of dots form characters and illustrations. They are noisy and very slow in comparison to inkjet and laser printers.

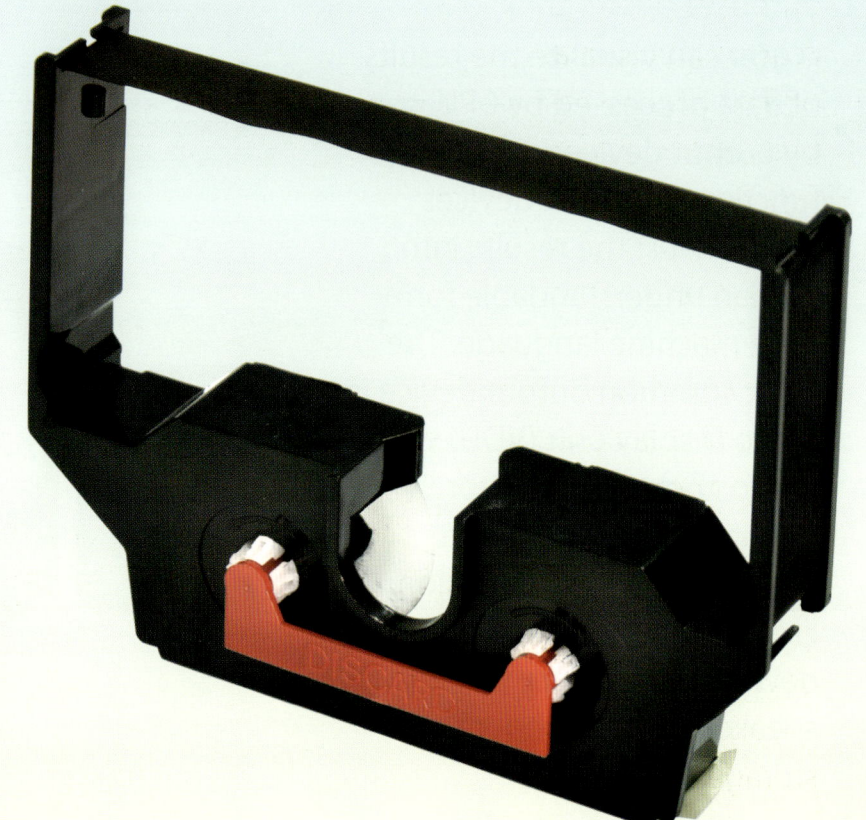

How does a computer work?

Inkjet printers work by propelling variably-sized droplets of liquid or molten material (ink) onto almost any medium. They are the most common type of printers for domestic purposes due to their low cost and high quality of output. These printers are very easy to use and handle. The main disadvantage is that the printing is slow, little noisy and non-economical.

onto paper. They produce high quality text and graphics on plain paper. The printing is fast and more economical than of inkjet printers.

Laser printers use LED-technology to obtain small particles of toner from a cartridge

19

COMPUTERS

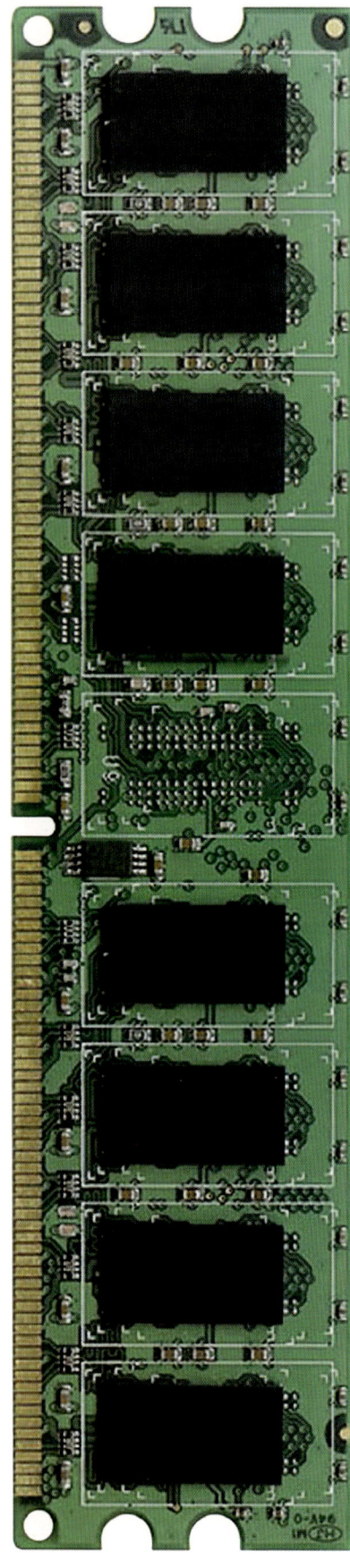

Computer memory

Computer memory is basically a place where data and instructions are stored in any form electronic, magnetic or optical. It is generally categorized into volatile memory and non-volatile memory according to the storage type. The volatile memory needs to be supplied with external power in order to hold and refresh data while a non-volatile memory can maintain data for extended periods of time without any power being supplied to the device. Thus, volatile memory is preferred for high-speed processing and short-term access while for long term storage and future access non-volatile memory is preferred. Random Access Memory (RAM) and Read Only Memory (ROM) constitute computers' internal memory as they are integrated part of processor circuit. The secondary storage devices like hard disk, magnetic tapes, zip drives, floppy disk drives and optical storage media are known as computer's external memory. They may or may not physically reside within processing unit but are not mounted on the main circuit.

Random access memory

Random access memory or RAM is the main memory of a computer system used for storing user instructions and data. It is volatile and provides temporary read/write storage. As soon as the power is turned off, all the data is lost. It is expensive and fast with access times generally less than nanoseconds. Every data and program is first stored in RAM for execution by CPU. RAM may be further divided into two categories:

How does a computer work?

Static random access memory (SRAM)

This type of RAM retains the data as long as power is available. It is fast and expensive and is used to create speed sensitive cache.

Dynamic random access memory (DRAM)

Dynamic RAM has to be dynamically refreshed all of the time. It is less expensive and slower and is used for larger RAM space requirements.

Read only memory

All computers contain a non-volatile read-only memory (ROM) that holds instructions for starting up the computer or a specific program. In general, ROM memory is used to hold and make available instructions that cannot be altered by users. Instructions are

> Did you know that 'Stewardesses' is the longest word which can be typed with only the left hand?

programmed into ROM memory during fabrication. According to data storage format, ROM can be divided into one-time programmable ROM (OTPROM), erasable programmable ROM (EPROM), electrically erasable programmable ROM (EEPROM) and many others.

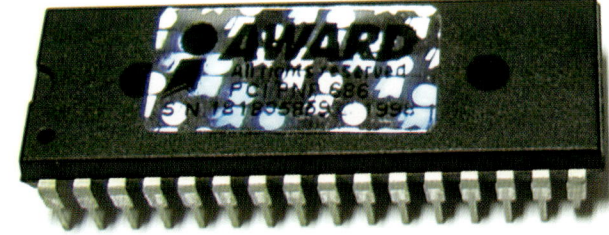

21

COMPUTERS

Secondary storage devices

The secondary storage is known as peripheral storage, and is used to store information of the computer that is not in current use. This is typically slower due to serial access and is of higher capacity than primary storage. The secondary storage devices are non-volatile. The common secondary storage devices are hard disks, optical drive such as CDs or DVDs and USB flash drives. The optical drives use lasers to store and read data on CDs and DVDs. USB flash drives are easily portable and have become incredibly popular due to the very small size compared to the amount of data these can store.

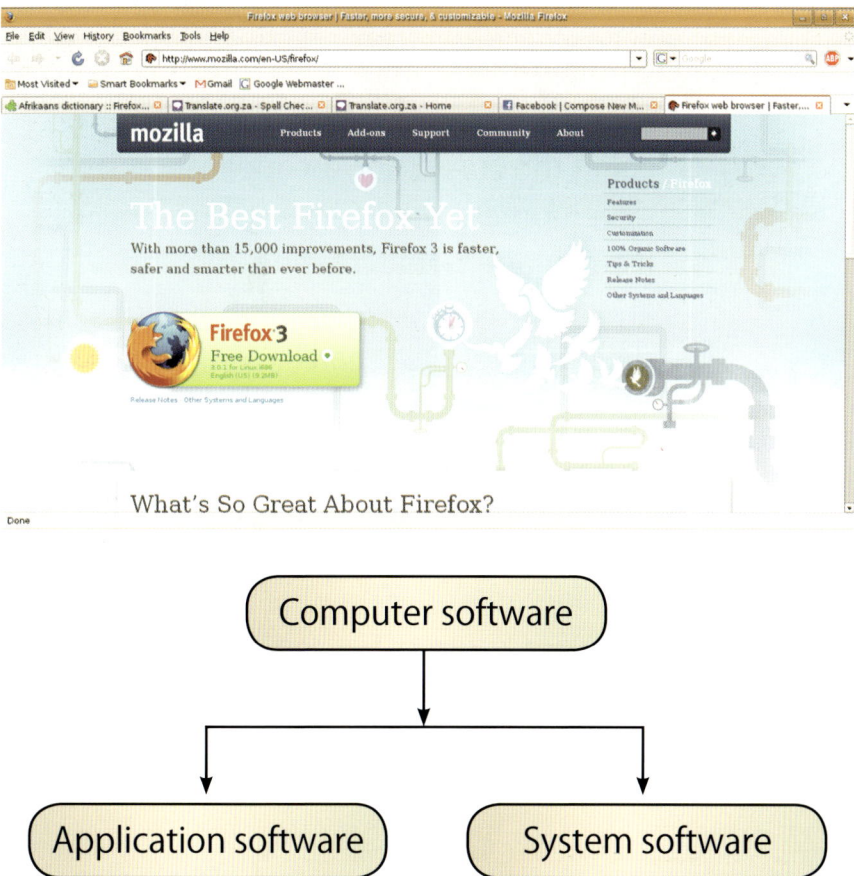

Computer Software are the programs are the intermediate link between computer system and user which aid to the proper functioning of the hardware of the computer system and support end user computing.

Application software

These are the programs developed for general-purpose or specific applications. These programs perform common information processing jobs for end users. Some of the common general-purpose programs are software suits, word processor, spreadsheet, web browsers, database managers, telecommunications, and graphics programs. Specific application programs include engineering and science applications for research and development purpose, educational and learning packages, statistical tools and business applications.

COMPUTERS

System software

These programs manage and support operations of a computer system for data processing tasks. System management programs manage the hardware, software, networks and other components of a computer system during its execution of information processing jobs. They include operating system, diagnostic tools, compilers, servers, data communication programs, database management systems, system utility programs and performance monitors etc. Development programs include the programming language tools and translators etc. The system utility programs support using the computer, an application or a development environment. They include file management (creating, moving and renaming folders, copying and deleting files), file search, comparing file contents. They also include software for performing diagnostic routines to check the performance and current health of the hardware. The operating system is considered as the head of the system software and most of the other system softwares are installed with it.

Operating systems

An operating system is integration of system programs that supervises and manages all of the CPU operations, controls the input/output storage functions of the computer system and provides various support services. It runs all the time and serves as the head of the computer system. It provides the environment where all the programs and software can only be executed. Thus, the basic function of an operating system is to create an interface between system and user. The popular operating systems are Windows 2000, XP, Windows 7, MS-DOS, Macintosh OS, OS/2, UNIX, Linux, Fedora, Ubuntu and many others.

> It is believed that the first computer virus released in the world was a boot sector virus, which was created in the year 1986 by Farooq Alvi brothers. It was designed by them to protect their research work.

COMPUTERS

Number system

We use decimal number system in our routine calculations. It has base 10 and all the numbers are represented by 10 digits (0, 1, 2, 3, 4, 5, 6, 7, 8 and 9). The commonly used number systems used by computers are binary, octal and hexadecimal. Most of the personal computer systems use binary number systems.

Binary number system has base 2 and the representing digits are 0 and 1. These digits are known as Binary Digits (BITS). **Octal number system** has base 8 and representing digits are 0-7 while **hexadecimal number system** has base 16 and representing symbols are 0-9 and A-F.

Measurement units of computer memory

Computer memory or storage capacity is measured by Binary Digits (0 and 1). This level of storage is termed as a bit (either 0 or 1).

1 byte = 8 bits
1 kilobyte (KB) = 1024 bytes
1 megabyte (MB) = 1024 kilobytes
1 gigabyte (GB) = 1024 megabyte
1 terabyte (TB) = 1024 gigabyte

How does a computer work?

Decimal	Binary	Octal	Hexadecimal
0	0	0	0
1	1	1	1
2	10	2	2
3	11	3	3
4	100	4	4
5	101	5	5
6	110	6	6
7	111	7	7
8	1000	10	8
9	1001	11	9
10	1010	12	A
11	1011	13	B
12	1100	14	C
13	1101	15	D
14	1110	16	E
15	1111	17	F

COMPUTERS

Internet

Internet is the network of networks which connects computer systems worldwide by various means such as telephone wires or satellite. The www (**World Wide Web**) is a network of sites that can be searched and retrieved by a special protocol known as a Hypertext Transfer protocol (HTTP). This protocol searches the address on the web and automatically retrieves for viewing.

Milestones to the discovery of Internet Technology

1973: The Internet technology was developed by Vinton Cerf in 1973 as part of a United States Department of Defense Advanced Research Projects Agency (DARPA) project. The computer network this project produced was called ARPANET that linked U.S. scientific and academic researchers.

1974: ARPA scientists, working closely with experts in Stanford, developed a common language that would allow different networks to communicate with each other. This was known as a transmission control protocol/internet protocol (TCP/IP).

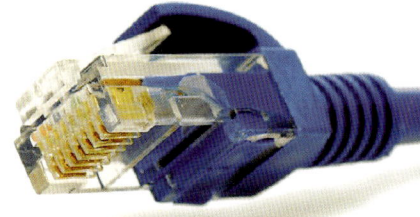

1989: Tim Berners-Lee and scientists at CERN (Geneva) designed **WWW concept** in 1989 for making data retrieval process easier. He also developed a 'browser/editor' program and called it **World Wide Web**.

1990: Archie, the first Internet search-engine for finding and retrieving computer files was developed at McGill University, Montreal.

1991: World Wide Web (internet) was released to the public.

How does the internet work?

Internet Network can be divided into two groups— servers and browsers. **Servers** store most of the information on the internet. They share this information with other servers and make it available for browsers. **Browsers** are standard computer systems which access the stored information on servers through web browsers. Some of the popular web browsers are Netscape Navigator, Microsoft Internet Explorer, Mozilla Firefox, Google Chrome and Opera etc.

COMPUTERS

Computer viruses

Computer viruses are the programs which are designed for self replication by infecting the executable files, system areas or storage media without the knowledge of the user. The most common mode of infection these days is internet. The actions and effects are most of the times considered bad ranging from mild disturbance to high damages to the system and its components. The notorious virus irritate users by flashing silly messages or product advertising while harmful virus can delete or corrupt important system files as well as stored data. The common types of virus are trojan horses, worms, parasites, hoaxes, macros, and boot sector viruses etc.

Trojan horses: These are malicious program codes which are not self-replicative. They are always spread in the form of good offers and once clicked; they spread rapidly and infect the complete system. These are one of the most common types of virus.

Hoaxes: These are the email messages carrying wrong information and instruction. Sometimes they are coded for self forwarding. Once these messages are opened, they are forwarded to everyone in the address book.

Boot sector viruses: These viruses install themselves on the beginning tracks of hard drives. They are malicious in nature and corrupt the device.

Test Your MEMORY

1. What are the main characteristics of a computer system?

2. Who is known as the father of computers and why?

3. What are the different types of computers?

4. What are the input and output devices?

5. Write a short note on Central Processing Unit?

6. What is the difference between volatile and non-volatile memories?

7. What are secondary storage devices?

8. Name some of the common operating system?

9. Classify the computer softwares.

10. How does the internet work?

11. What are the different types of printers?

12. What are the common types of computer viruses?

Index

A

Abacus 5
Address Bus 16
Analog computers 9
analytic engine 6
Application software 23
ARPANET 28

B

Binary number system 26
BITS 26
boot sector viruses 30

C

calculating machine 6
central processing unit 12
computer software 23
computer viruses 30
Control Bus 16

D

Data Bus 16
decimal number system 26
Dynamic random access
       memory 21

H

hard disk 13, 20
hardware 23, 24

I

input device 12, 13
integrated circuits 14
internal buses 14
internal memory 20
Internet 4, 28, 29, 30

K

keyboard 12, 13

L

light pen 13
Linux 25
logarithms 5
logic unit 14

M

Macintosh OS 25
macros 30
Mark I 7
memory unit 14
microphones 13
microprocessor 14
monitor 12, 17
mouse 13
MS-DOS 25

N

non-volatile memory 20

O

operating system 24, 25
output device 12, 17

P

parallel processing 11
PARAM 11

R

Random Access Memory 20
Read Only Memory 20

S

spreadsheet 23
storage device 12
super computers 11
system software 24
system utility programs 24

T

Tabulating Machine 7
translators 24

V

Visualizing Display Unit 12

W

word processor 23

PEGASUS ENCYCLOPEDIA LIBRARY

DISCOVERIES AND INVENTIONS
DISCOVERIES

Edited by: Anil Kumar Tomar, Pallabi B. Tomar
Managing editor: Tapasi De
Designed by: Vijesh Chahal, Anil Kumar, Rohit Kumar
Illustrated by: Suman S. Roy, Tanoy Choudhury
Colouring done by: Vinay Kumar, Sonu, Kiran Kumari & Pradeep Kumar

DISCOVERIES

CONTENTS

What do we mean by a discovery? 3
The universe and planets 4
Blood circulation 5
The cell 6
Fire 8
Newton's Laws of Motion 9
Photosynthesis 11
Oxygen 12
Atomic Theory 13
The Saturn's Ring 14
Anaesthesia 15
Darwin's theory of evolution 16
Boyle's law of ideal gas 17
Rainbow—dispersion of light 18
Law of conservation of mass 19
Subatomic particles 20
The Nucleus 22
The Neutron 23
Vitamins 24
Fossils of dinosaurs 25
Radioactive Dating 26
Blood Transfusion 27
Penicillin 28
X-rays 29
Human Immunodeficiency Virus (HIV) 30
Test Your Memory 31
Index 32

What do we mean by a discovery?

Discoveries and inventions are used most of the times as synonyms but they are two different terms. A discovery refers to something which already exists, but which has been found by someone for the first time. An invention is something a man has produced quite new and which did not exist before.

For example, the blood circulation system in the human body existed since the existence of humans and it was discovered by William Harvey. This system could not be invented because it already existed.

Barometer was invented by Evangelista Torricelli to measure the atmospheric pressure. Barometer could not be discovered as it did not exist in the nature.

This book highlights some of the greatest discoveries of the world.

DISCOVERIES

The universe and planets

Everything that exists is the part of the universe. The galaxies are the biggest components of the universe each consisting of billions of stars. Each star has its solar system in which planets revolve around it. Our solar system, which consists of Earth and eight other planets revolving around the sun in an elliptical path, is embedded in Milky Way galaxy. The big bang theory explains the origin of universe and the way it is expanding. According to this theory, the universe is formed by expansion of an extremely dense and hot state and is continuously expanding.

Nicolaus Copernicus in 1543 ruled out all the previous assumptions about Earth, sun and stars. He placed the sun at the centre of the solar system and said

Solar system

Earth is not static but it moves around the sun. In early 17th century, Galileo Galilei discovered that Jupiter also has moons. Edwin Hubble (1924-1929) discovered for the first time that the universe is expanding. He also proved this by his experimental calculations and found that the galaxies which are farther from our galaxy are moving away with faster speed.

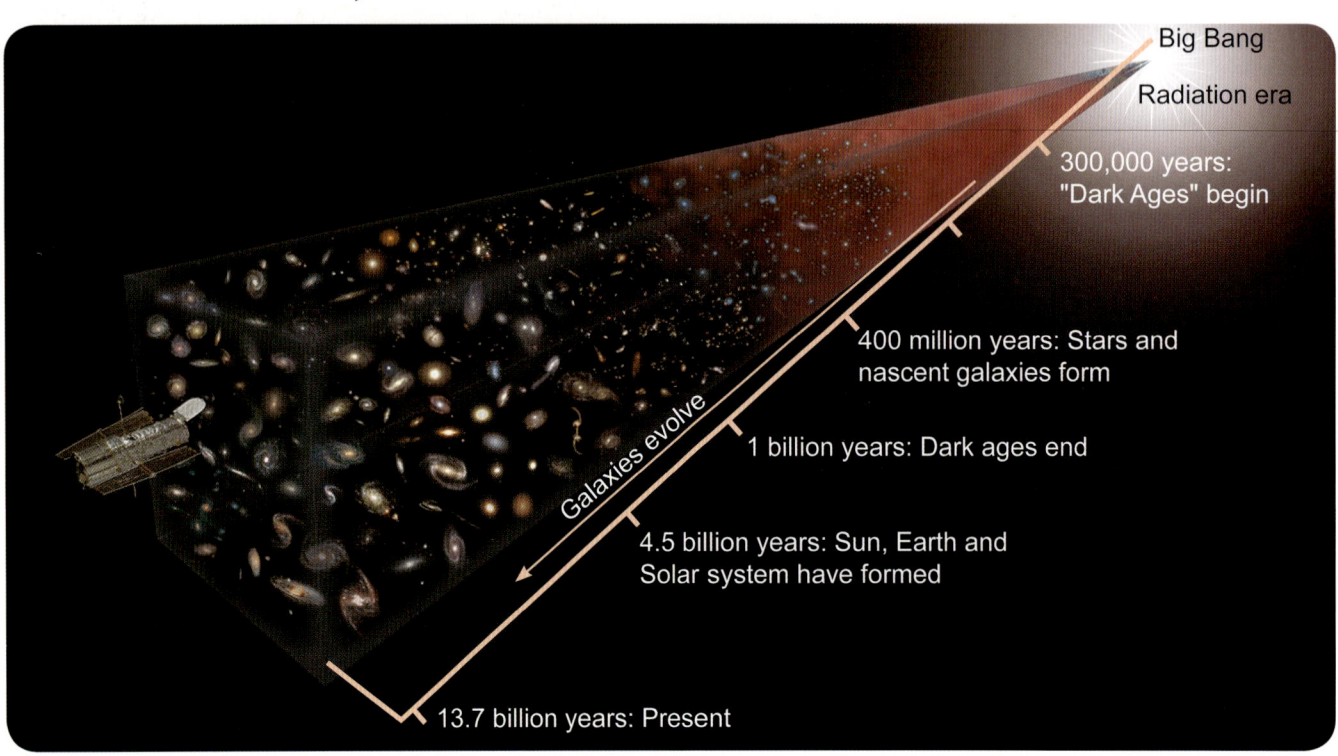
Big bang

Blood circulation

William Harvey, an English physician and anatomist discovered the circulation of the blood in 1628. He published his findings in *'Exercitatio Anatomica de Motu Cordis et Sanguinis in Animalibus'* (Anatomical Essay on the Motion of the Heart and Blood in Animals). This finding marks the beginning of modern physiology. During his experiments, Harvey observed that blood entered the right side of the heart and it was forced into the lungs before returning to the left side of the heart. From left heart, blood was pumped through the aorta into the arteries around the body. The detailed analysis made him realize that the amount of blood flowing through this system was too much for the liver to produce. Thus, he deduced that there is a blood circulation system and heart plays an important role to circulate blood through the system. Though he didn't observe blood capillaries as there was no microscope but he proposed the existence of tiny vessels that linked the arteries to the veins.

William Harvey

DISCOVERIES

The cell

The cell, basic building block of all forms of life is the smallest unit which can be biologically defined as being alive. It was discovered in 1665 by an English scientist Robert Hooke. He was examining a dried thin section of a cork under a light microscope and discovered empty spaces contained by walls. He termed them pores or cells and was later credited for discovering the building blocks of all life. He recorded all his observations of small bodies visualized under his microscope into **Micrographia**. Robert Hooke described the cells as containers for the noble plant juices of the living cork tree. He also believed that cells existed only in plants since these structures were observed only in plant materials.

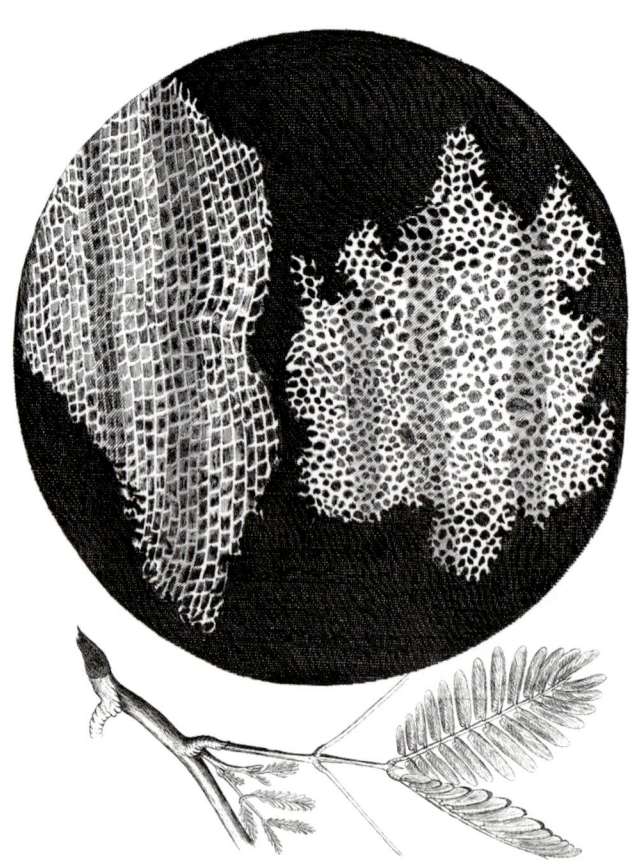

The cell Nucleus

For more than 100 years, it was believed that the cells could not further be subdivided. In 1831, an eminent Scottish botanist Robert Brown identified an opaque spot within the cells while he was observing the epidermis of a collection of orchids with his microscope. He used the term areola to describe them. He also observed this spot during the early stage of pollen formation. This made him conclude that this spot is key components of all cells and termed it as **nucleus**.

Robert Hooke

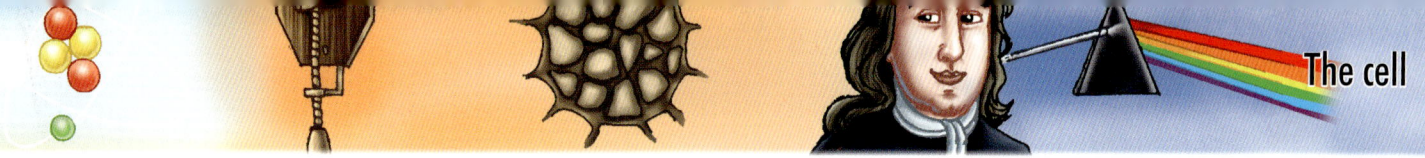

The cell

The cell theory

Various observations later revealed that cell is the basic building block of all living organisms and the cell theory came into existence. The cell theory was proposed by the German Scientists Jacob Schleiden and Theodore Schwann for the first time in 1838 and formalized by Rudolf Virchow in 1858.

The modern cell theory states that:

1. The cell is the basic structural and functional unit of life. All living organisms are composed of cells whether unicellular or multicellular.

2. All cells arise from preexisting cells. Each cell contains genetic material that is passed down during this process.

3. All basic chemical and physiological functions take place inside cells and activities of cells depend on the activities of sub cellular structures within the cell.

Plant Cell Structure

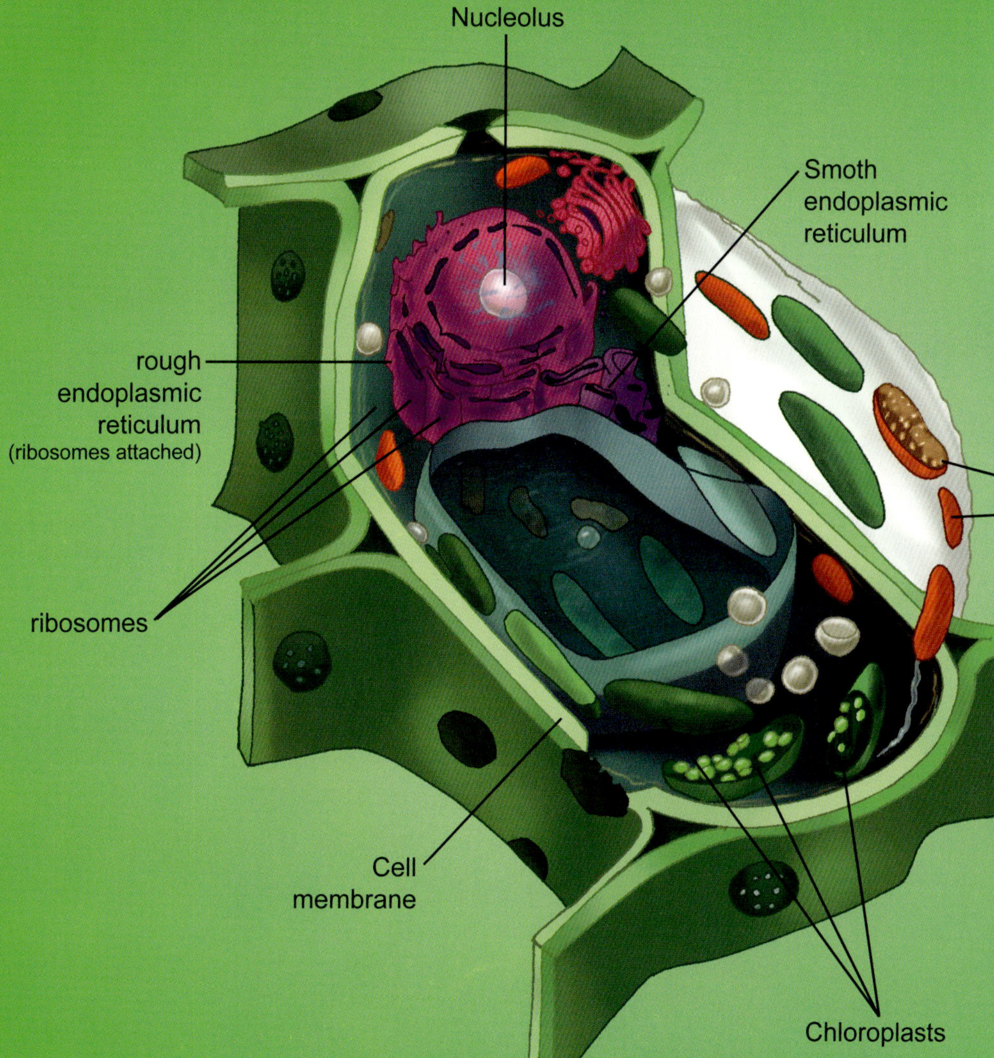

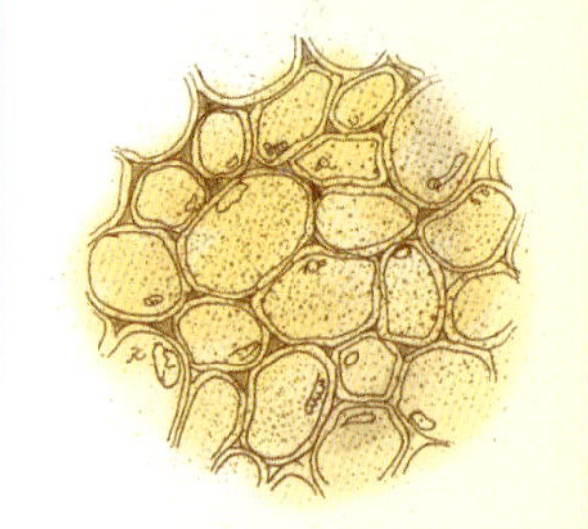

Labels: Nucleolus, Smoth endoplasmic reticulum, rough endoplasmic reticulum (ribosomes attached), ribosomes, Cell membrane, Chloroplasts, Mitochondrian

Plant tissue (consisting of many cells)

DISCOVERIES

Fire

Fire was undoubtedly one of our earliest gifts from nature. Human beings have known how to make and control fire since very ancient times. We do have evidence of hearths in caves dating back to almost a hundred thousand years ago in the dwellings of the Neanderthal Man. How this was first accomplished is shrouded in mystery, as indeed are so many other details pertaining to practically every initial giant step in human history. The creation of fire could well have been a chance discovery. Early

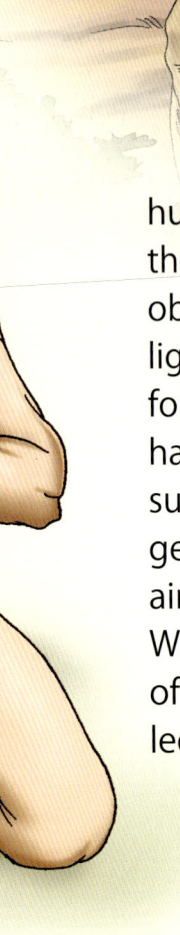

humans were certainly familiar with the heat of the sun. They must have observed lightning flashes. A powerful lightning could have set a tree or a forest ablaze or a dry leaf or twig may have caught fire in the open, on a hot summer day. A human being may have generated sparks quite accidentally by aimless rubbing or scratching stones. With the discovery of ways of making of fire, men started cooking and this led to the human civilization.

Newton's Laws of Motion

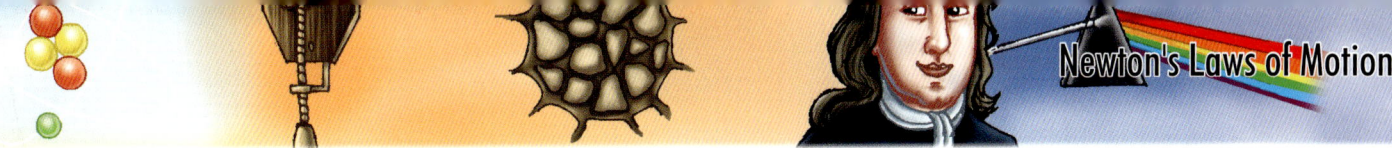

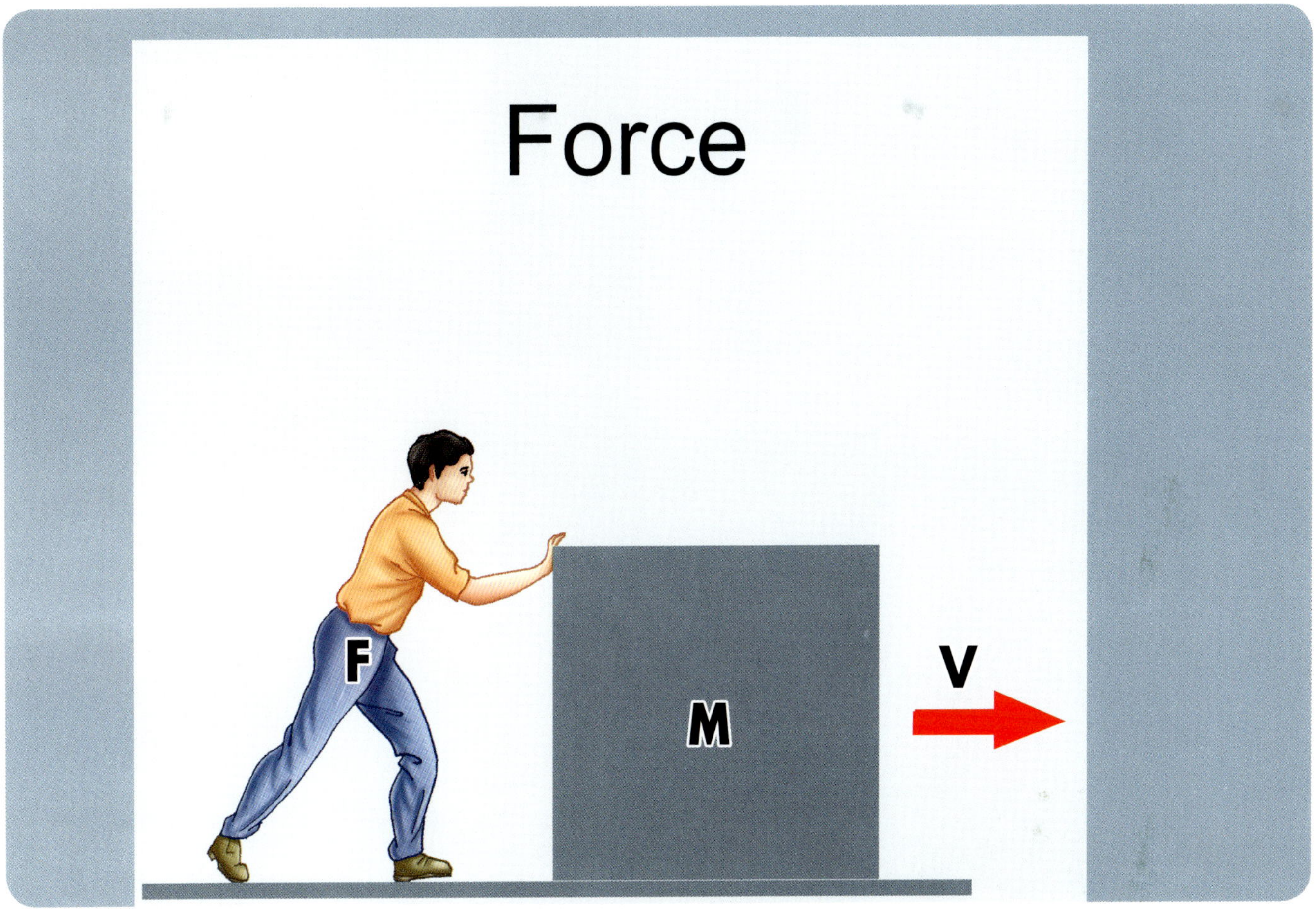

Isaac Newton was one of the greatest scientists of all the times in human history. He was an English physicist, mathematician, astronomer and philosopher. In 1687, he formulated three laws to describe the movement of objects which are the foundation of classical mechanics. The first, second and third laws are commonly known as **law of inertia**, **law of force** and **law of reciprocal actions** respectively.

Law of inertia: All bodies tend to remain at rest or to maintain a constant direction and speed, until some external force is not applied.

Law of force: If some external force is applied to a body, it produces acceleration in the direction of the applied force. The product of the acceleration and the mass of the object is equal to the force applied.

Law of reciprocal actions: For every action there is an equal and opposite reaction.

DISCOVERIES

Newton published **Philosophiae Naturalis Principia Mathematica (or Principia)** in 1687. This book explains Newton's three laws of motion and Universal law of gravitation.

The universal law of gravitation states that every particle of matter in the universe attracts every other particle with a force. This force acts along the line joining their centres and is directly proportional to the product of their masses and inversely proportional to the square of the distance between them.

Isaac Newton

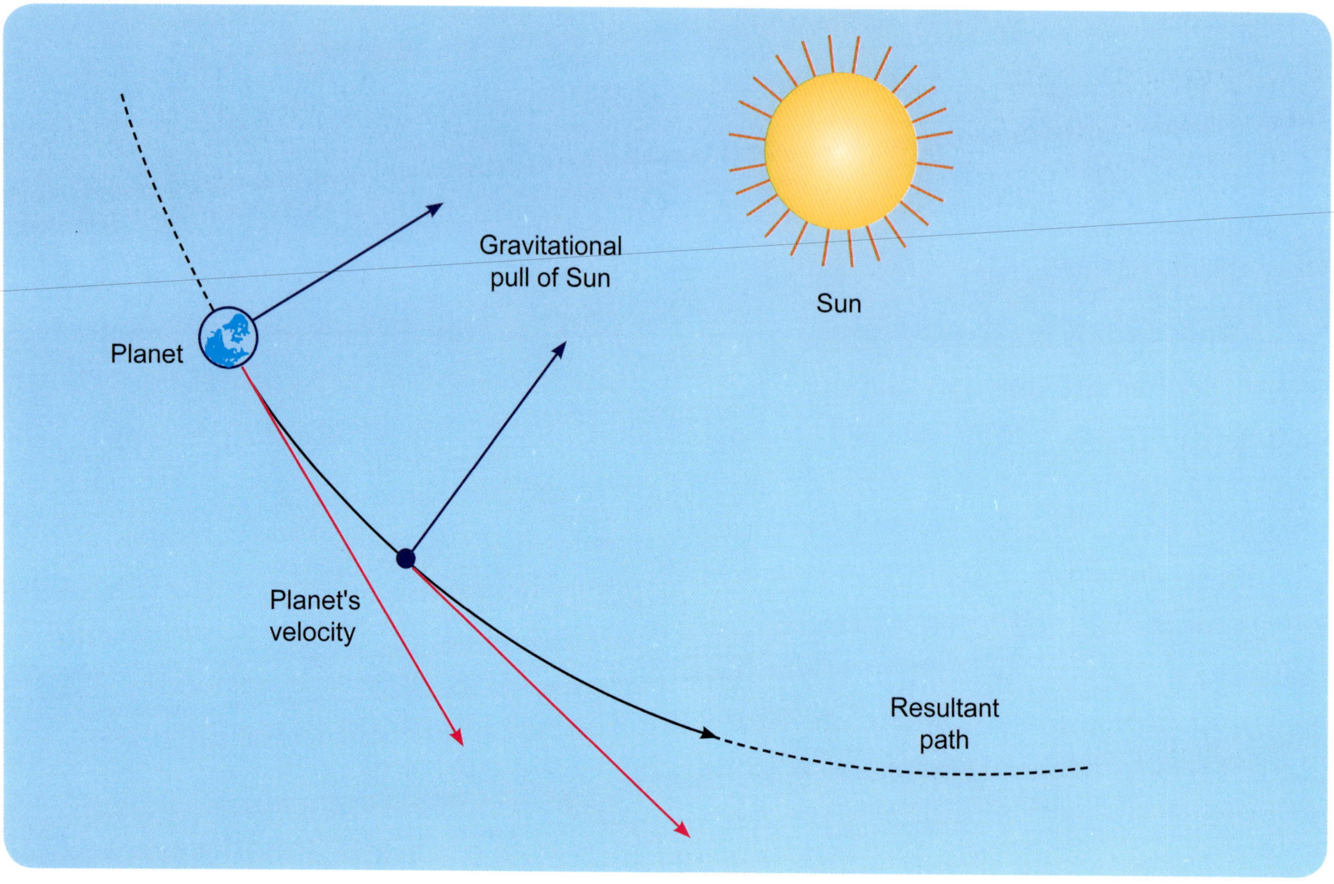

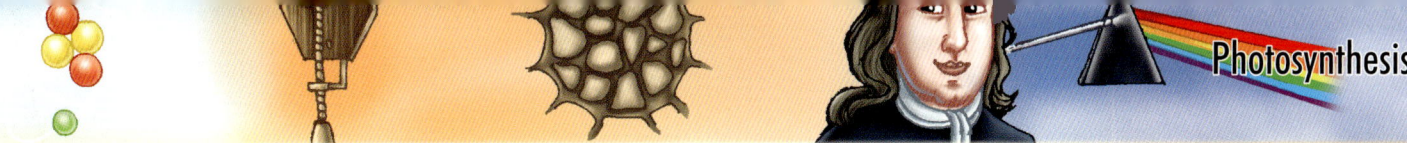

Photosynthesis

Plants, algae and some bacteria convert the light energy of the sun into the chemical energy through the process known as photosynthesis. The plants use captured sunlight to convert water and carbon dioxide into sugars like glucose. The process occurs in the chloroplasts and uses the green pigment of plants, chlorophyll. Thus, the basic ingredients of photosynthesis are carbon dioxide, water, chlorophyll and sunlight. The ancient Greek philosophers believed that plants obtained all of their nutrients from the soil. In the 17th century, Jan Baptista van Helmont, a Dutch physician and chemist performed experiments by growing a willow tree and concluded that the tree gained the weight from the water he added to the soil. Though he did not understand the process and its gradients but his experiments advanced the understanding of photosynthesis.

Julius Mayer

In 1771, Joseph Priestley implicated the role of atmospheric gases in plant growth. Jan Ingenhousz, a Dutch physician discovered that plants react to sunlight differently than shade. Through a series of experiments, he demonstrated that green parts of plants cleaned the air only when placed in strong light. In 1796, he also suggested that this process of photosynthesis causes carbon dioxide to split into carbon and oxygen and oxygen is released as a gas.

In 1804, the Swiss scientists, Nicholas Theodore de Saussure carefully measured the amounts of carbon dioxide and water that were given to the plant. He showed that the carbon in the plants came from carbon dioxide and the hydrogen from water. Finally in 1844, a German scientist, Julius Mayer, showed that the energy of sunlight is captured in photosynthesis.

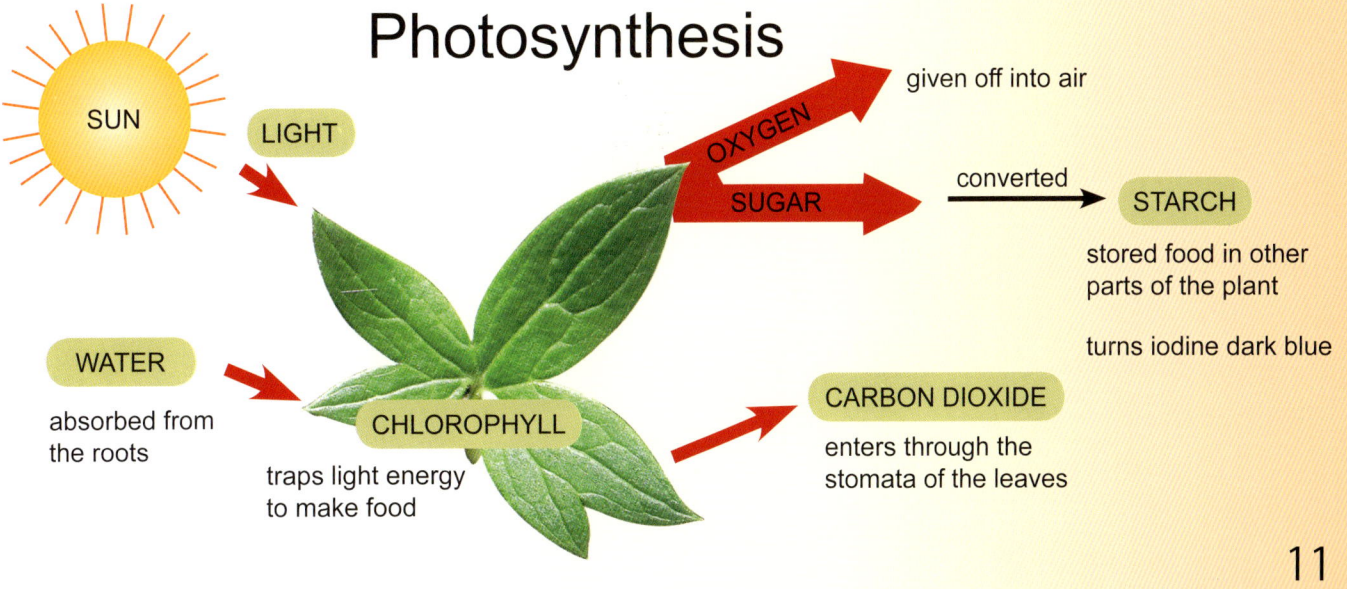

Oxygen

Life on Earth cannot be imagined without oxygen. Animals and plants require it for respiration and to survive. It is tasteless, colourless and odourless gaseous element. It is the third most abundant element of the universe. It constitutes almost 21 per cent of the Earth's atmosphere and half of the Earth's crust. Oxygen is commonly used in oxidizers, rocket propulsion, medicines, welding, sensors, oxygen masks and concentrators.

Joseph Priestley

British chemist Joseph Priestley and the Swedish chemist Carl Wilhelm Scheele are credited for the discovery of oxygen by isolating oxygen in the gaseous state. Scheele was the first scientist who discovered oxygen in 1771 but it was Priestley who discovered oxygen in 1774 and proved that oxygen was essential to combustion and respiration. He published his findings in the same year and called the new gas 'dephlogisticated air'. The carbonated water, hydrochloric acid, nitrous oxide (commonly known as laughing gas), carbon monoxide and sulphur dioxide were also discovered by him. The name 'oxygen' was coined by a French chemist, Antoine Lavoisier in 1775. He was the first scientist who recognized oxygen as an element, characterized it and described its role in combustion.

Atomic Theory

Atomic theory is one of the greatest scientific discoveries of the 19th Century which marks the beginning of modern chemistry. A British school teacher, John Dalton, formulated this theory in the year 1803. For the first time in history, he recognized the difference between atom and compounds. This theory is based on his experiments and laws of chemical combinations.

Main postulates of Dalton's atomic theory are:

1) All matter is made of indivisible and indestructible particles called atoms.

2) All atoms of the same element are identical in mass and properties but they differ from the atoms of other elements.

3) Compounds are formed by a combination of atoms of two or more elements in a fixed whole number ratio.

4) Atoms are the smallest unit of matter and a chemical reaction is a rearrangement of atoms.

Though this theory many drawbacks and its assumptions were proved wrong but it enabled us to explain the laws of chemical combination.

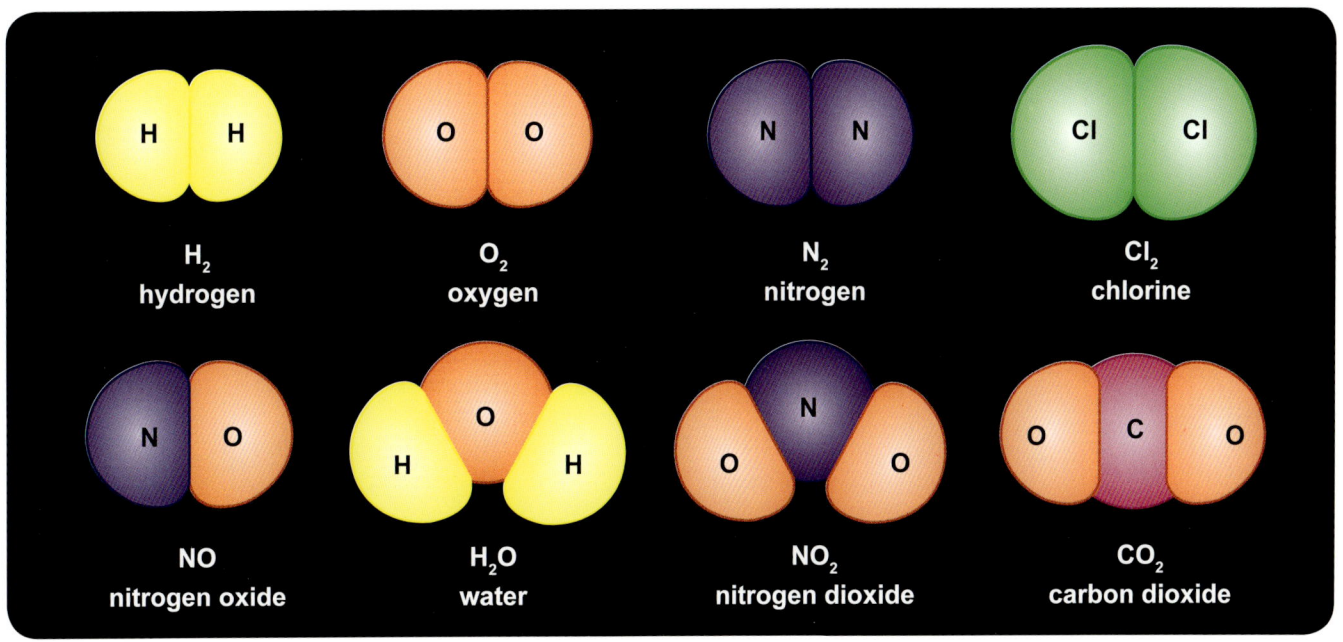

DISCOVERIES

The Saturn's Ring

In 1610, Galileo Galilei observed a bright star flanked by two dimmer ones with his primitive telescope. He was amazed with the fact that the star he observed was not a single star, but three together, which almost touched each other. What he had discovered was a planet that was to become one of the wonders of the solar system. This planet was later named 'Saturn'. Saturn's beauty comes from its magnificent rings. Galileo described them as 'handles' or large moons on either side of the planet. Galileo's discovery of Saturn commenced the scientific process of unravelling the mysteries of Saturn's extensive ring system. But even after 400 years the mysteries have not been all solved. In 1655, Christann Huyges proposed that Saturn was surrounded by

a solid ring. He described this ring as a thin and flat ring which nowhere touched the Saturn and was inclined to the ecliptic. As time went on, more and more observations were made and theories proposed. According to the modern prominent theories, the ring is made out of small particles rather than being solid.

Anaesthesia

Anaesthesia is used to produce a condition in the body of having sensation blocked or temporarily taken away. This allows patients to undergo surgery and other procedures without the distress and pain they would otherwise experience. The discovery of surgical anaesthesia in the early 1840s represented a unique American contribution to medicine. The word anaesthesia was coined by Oliver Wendell Holmes, Sr. in 1846.

Before the mid 1800's a person undergoing surgery was in for a terrifying time. In those pre-anaesthetic days, there was nothing to dull the pain but whiskey. Attempts to dull the pain of patients led to the use of marijuana, opium and hashish in China and India. In the 1840s ether became popular for recreational use. One day an American physician by the name of Crawford W. Long noted that people under the influence of ether felt no pain. He immediately realised the potential to relieve the pain of surgery.

The first operation using ether as an anaesthetic took place on March 30th, 1842. Later, nitrous oxide (laughing gas) and Chloroform were also used as anaesthesia. Advancements were made that allowed a patient to remain awake while a specific part of their body was made anaesthetic.

DISCOVERIES

Darwin's theory of evolution

Charles Darwin

The theory of evolution is one of the greatest scientific revolutions of human history. It drastically changed our perception of the world and of our place in it. Charles Darwin put forth a coherent theory of evolution and gathered a great body of evidence in support of this theory. Darwin's Theory of Evolution is the widely held notion that all life is related and has descended from a common ancestor; that is, the birds and the bananas, the fishes and the flowers, all have common ancestors. According to Darwin's theory, the development of life from non-life and stresses a purely naturalistic 'descent with modification'. That is, complex creatures evolve from more simplistic ancestors naturally over time. He also suggested that random genetic mutations occur within an organism's genetic code and the beneficial mutations are preserved because they aid survival. This process is known as 'natural selection'. These beneficial mutations are passed on to the next generation. Over the time, beneficial mutations accumulate and the result is an entirely different organism. The new organism maybe a variation of the original or an entirely different creature.

Boyle's law of ideal gas

Robert Boyle (1627-1691) was an Irish-born philosopher who did research and investigation in physics, chemistry and theology. Boyle is known as the founder of modern chemistry because he believed in the intrinsic value of chemistry, developed the rigorous experimental scientific method and defined the element. In 1962, he proved his law for both great and small pressures and discovered a law of ideal gases. This law states that if we keep the temperature constant, pressure is inversely proportional to the volume. In simple words, pressure increases as volume decreases and pressure

DISCOVERIES

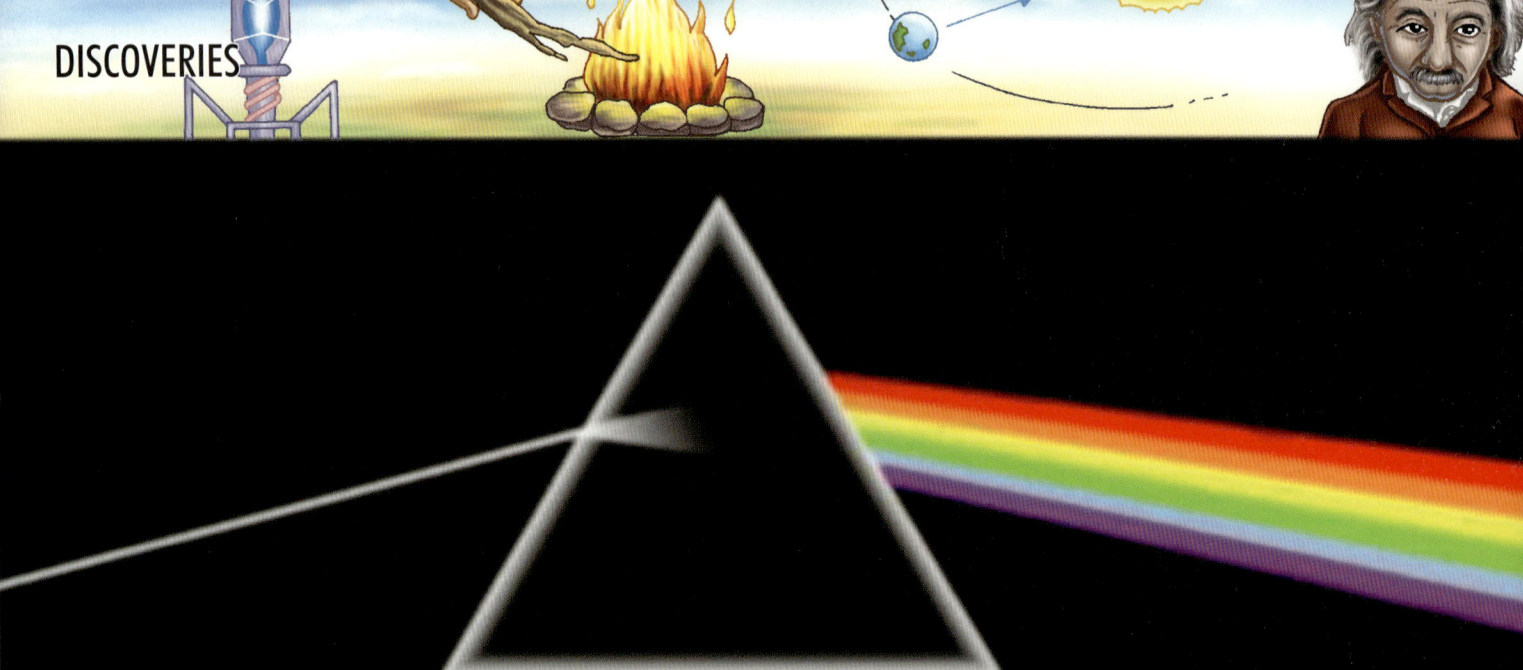

Rainbow—dispersion of light

Dispersion is the separation of a beam of light into its constituent colours. This takes place when a light beam passes through a dispersive medium. The sunlight is often called white light as it constitutes all the visible colours. It disperses into a spectra of seven colours when passes through a glass prism. In 1666, Sir Isaac Newton used a prism to disperse white light and discovered the constituent colours of white light. When light passes through a prism, it passes through two interfaces between glass and air. The light bends towards the normal when it enters the prism and away from the normal when it exits. As the two interfaces are at an angle, the dispersion is very easy to observe. The seven colours of white light are violet, indigo, blue, green, yellow, orange and red.

A well-known example of dispersion is the formation of a rainbow. A rainbow is formed when white light is dispersed through raindrops. Tiny droplets of water refract the white light from the sun and create a spectrum of colours similar to what happens in a prism. Since the droplets are spheres, the light is reflected internally in the droplets and the spectrum or rainbow returns toward the direction of the light. That is why the sun is always behind us when we see a rainbow.

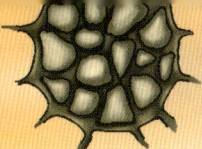

Law of conservation of mass

The law of conservation of mass states that the mass of substances in a closed system will remain constant, no matter what processes are acting inside the system. This universally accepted law explains that the matter may change from one form to another but it can neither be created nor destroyed. The mass of the reactants must always equal the mass of the products. This law was first formulated by Antoine Lavoisier in 1789. Some evidences also highlight that Mikhail Lomonosov, in 1748, had also expressed similar ideas. Thus, this law is commonly known as the Lomonosov-Lavoisier law. This law was the key to making chemistry into a real science which marked the beginning of modern chemistry. After this, the ideas of chemical elements, process of fire and oxidation and many other basic chemical principles could be better understood. In most situations the law of conservation of mass can be assumed valid. This law works fine for anything except for the matter that is approaching the speed of light. At high speeds, mass begins transforming to energy. Due to this reason, we now have the Law of Conservation of Mass and Energy.

Antoine Lavoisier

DISCOVERIES

Subatomic particles

Atoms are made up of three particles- electron, proton and neutron. Hydrogen atom is an exception as it does not have any neutron. The nucleus of an atom makes up the most of an atom's mass and consists of protons and neutrons. The electrons are smaller particles and revolve around the nucleus. The protons and electrons have positive and negative charges respectively while the neutrons are electrically neutral. An atom has the same number of electrons and protons to make it electrically neutral.

The Electron

Dalton's atomic theory stated that atoms make up all matter in the universe and they were, by definition, indivisible. But even before the entire scientific community accepted the facts of this theory, scientists disapproved the fact that atoms are indivisible. They believed that atoms were made up of even smaller entities.

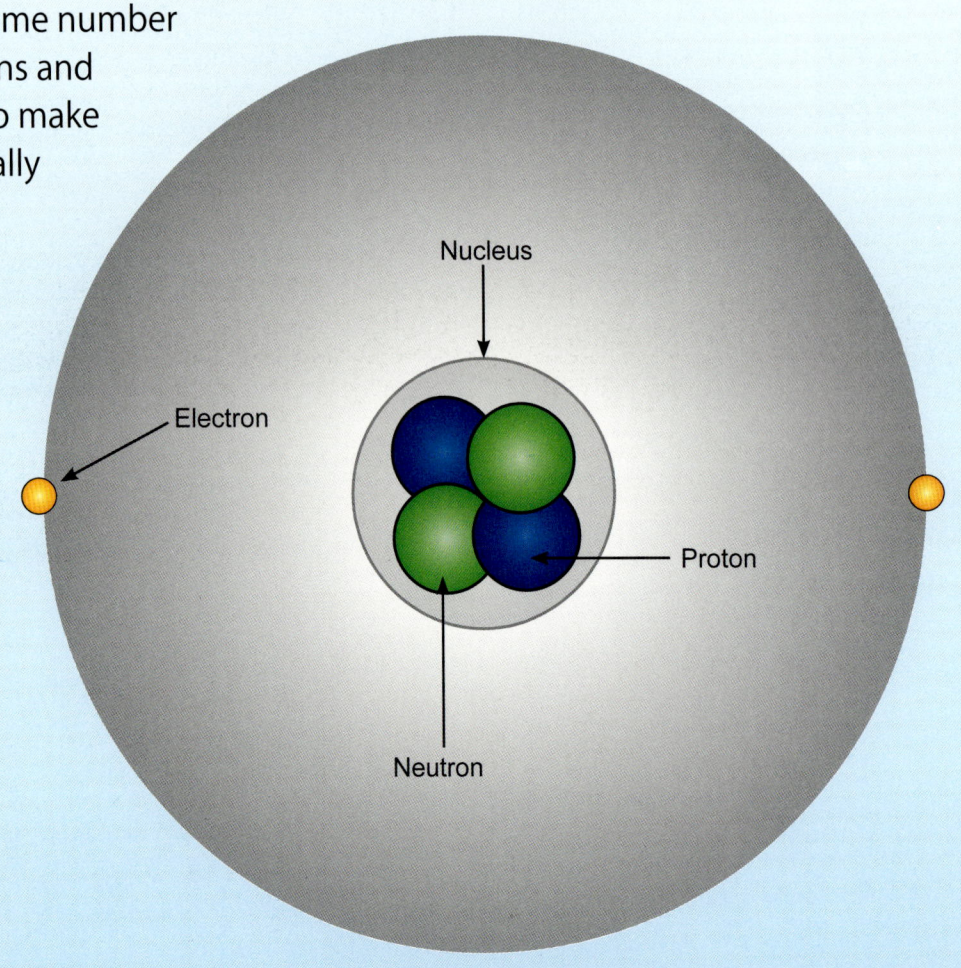

Subatomic particles

J.J. Thompson

In 1897, the British Physicist J.J. Thompson discovered the first subatomic particle – the electron while he was experimenting with a cathode ray tube at Cambridge University. He was working to find the constituent particles of cathode rays. In his experiment, he was able to bend the ray using a magnetic field and measured the direction in which the ray bent to determine both mass and charge. Based on his experiments, he proposed that something smaller than an atom existed in the form of tiny negatively charged particles.

Now it is well established that electrons are fundamental aspects of the atomic structure and they provide necessary charge to neutralize the atomic structure. The molecules are formed by combinations of atoms and these combinations are only possible by the bonds formed by electrons. An electron has a mass of 9.11×10^{-31} kg and a charge equal to 1.602×10^{-19} coulomb.

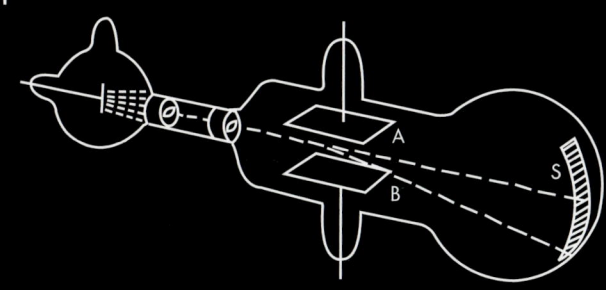

The Nucleus

The positively charged nucleus of an atom was discovered by New Zealand physicist Ernest Rutherford in 1909 during the Gold Foil experiment. This experiment was performed by Hans Geiger and Ernest Marsden at the University of Manchester under his guidance. In this experiment, positively charged alpha particles were fired at a high velocity into a very thin sheet of gold foil. The trajectories of these particles after passing through the foil were then detected and analyzed. Most of the alpha particles travelled straight through the foil with little or no deviation and a small fraction rebounded, ending up on the same side of the foil as the incoming beam. Based on these observations, Rutherford proposed new atomic model which states that negatively charged electrons orbited around a positively charged and incredibly dense central 'nucleus'. Through a series of experiments in 1918, Rutherford discovered that the positively charged particles were known as the proton. He also deduced that they are subatomic particles and the atom is divisible.

Ernest Rutherford

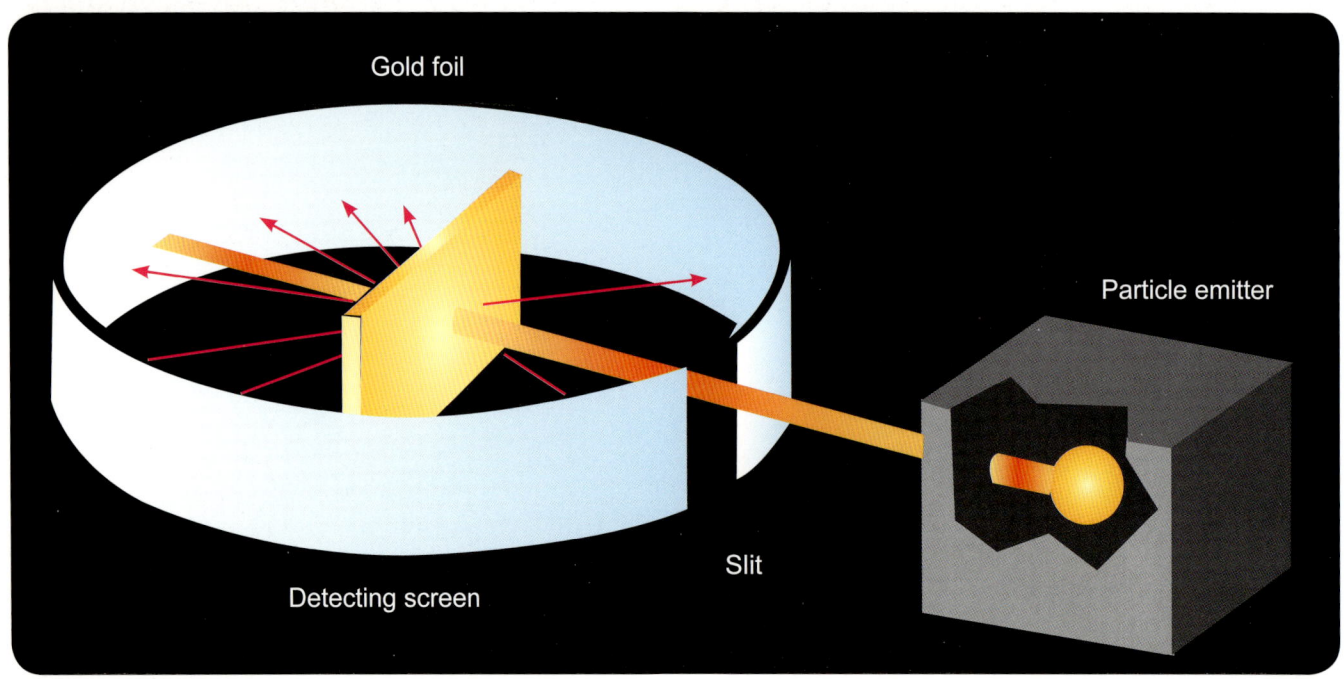

The Neutron

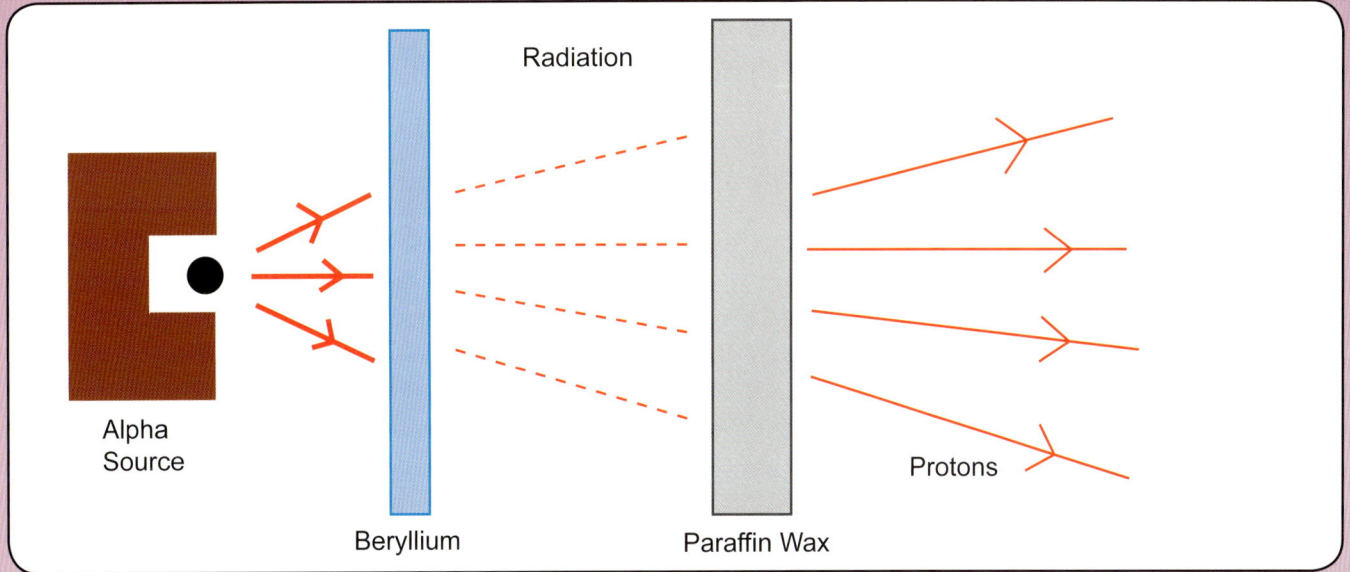

The neutron was discovered by James Chadwick in 1932. He bombarded beryllium (Be) with alpha particles and allowed the radiation emitted by beryllium to incident on a paraffin wax. It was found that protons were scattered out from the paraffin wax. He analyzed the scattered data and proved that the radiation consisted of neutral particles of mass approximately equal to that of proton. These neutral particles were named neutrons. Sir Chadwick was awarded with Noble Prize of Physics for his findings in 1935.

This discovery marked the adoption of the Rutherford-Bohr model of the atom. The main assumptions of this model are:

1. The nucleus of an atom is made up of protons and neutrons which are bound together by strong nuclear forces.
2. Electrons orbit the nucleus in the fixed shells.
3. Electrons and protons carry equal but opposite charges. The number of electrons and protons is the same in a neutral atom.

James Chadwick

DISCOVERIES

Vitamins

Vitamins are natural substances which are essential nutrients for humans. Deficiency of vitamins makes humans sick. To stay healthy, we need food rich in all type of vitamins as most of the vitamins (except vitamin D & K) cannot be synthesized by our body. In 1905, an English scientist William Fletcher while searching for the cause of disease Beriberi discovered that eating unpolished rice prevented Beriberi and eating polished rice did not. He suggested that there were some special factors or nutrients in the husk of the rice and if they were removed from food, disease is caused. In 1906, Sir Frederick Gowland Hopkins also discovered that some food factors were important to health. The term 'vitamine' was coined by Polish scientist Cashmir Funk in 1912 for these special nutritional parts of food. The name was later shortened to vitamin.

Fossils of dinosaurs

Dinosaurs are a diverse group of extinct animals that were the dominant terrestrial vertebrates for over 160 million years, from the late Triassic period until the end of the Cretaceous. A British fossil finder William Buckland discovered the first dinosaur fossil remains of our modern times. In 1819, Buckland discovered the Megalosaurus Bucklandii (Buckland's Giant Lizard) in England. It was given its name in 1824. Prior to this, Reverend Plot had found a huge femur bone as early as 1676 in England. It was thought to belong to a giant. Many anthropologists suggested that it might have belonged to a dinosaur. However, with the discovery of giant human skeletal remains ranging from 8 ft to 12 ft tall around the world in the last few hundred years, many believe the Plot femur may have belonged to a very tall human. In 1838, William Parker Foulke found the first complete dinosaur fossil in New Jersey, USA. Since Buckland's original discovery in 1819, hundreds of different dinosaur genera have been discovered so far.

DISCOVERIES

Radioactive Dating

The age of Earth has been a topic of long debate throughout the scientific community. Bertram Boltwood, an American chemist, discovered the method to calculate the age of a rock in 1907 by measuring the rate of Uranium-238 radioactive decay. Boltwood proposed that the age of a rock containing Uranium-238 can be determined by measuring the remaining amount of uranium-238 and the relative amount of the decaying product lead-206. Using his method, he estimated the age of Earth to be 2.2 billion years.

Radioactive dating methods are based on the disintegration property of radioactive substances. These substances eventually decay during the course of time into the stable nuclides. If the rate of decay is known, we can determine the age of a specimen containing radioactive substance by estimating the relative proportions of the remaining radioactive substance and the product of its decay. Carbon-14, Uranium-235, Uranium-238 and Thorium-232 are some of the common radioactive substances with approximate half life of 5730 years, 700 million years, 4.5 billion years and 14 billion years respectively.

Blood transfusion

Blood transfusion can be life-saving and necessary in the cases of extreme blood loss due to trauma or can be used to replace blood lost during surgery. Blood transfusions may also be used to treat a severe anaemia or other blood diseases. People suffering from haemophilia or sickle-cell anaemia disease may require frequent blood transfusions. Blood transfusions, in early times, used whole blood, but modern strategy is to use only components of the blood. Knowledge of the different blood types is crucial for safe blood transfusions. The most accepted blood classification is ABO system according to which all humans have one of the following four blood groups – A, B, AB or O. In 1901, an Austrian biologist Karl Landsteiner and his group discovered blood groups and developed a system of classification. For his discovery he was awarded the Nobel Prize in Medicine in 1930. He is also credited for discovering blood antigens and antibodies, specific to the blood groups.

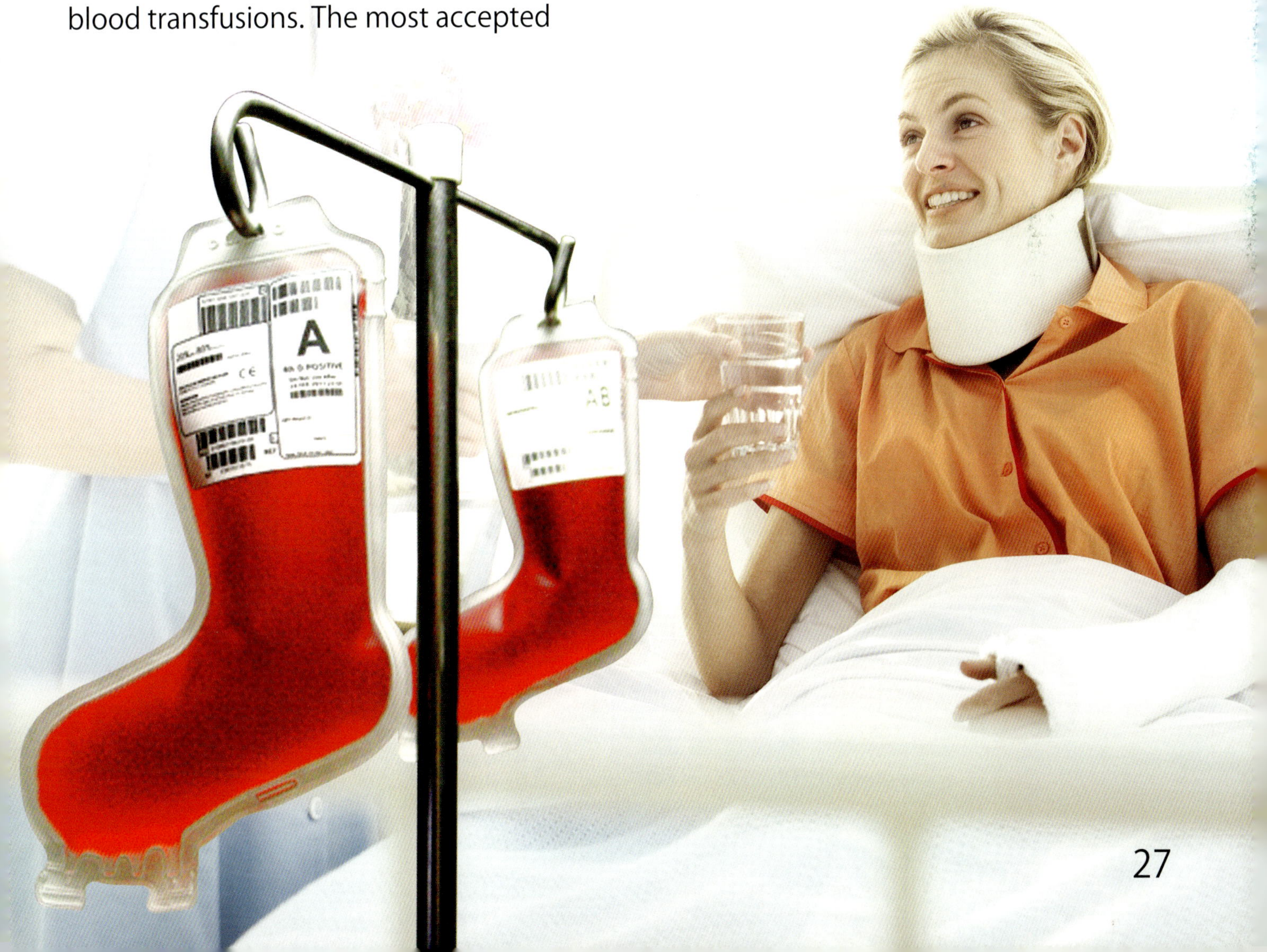

Penicillin

Alexander Fleming

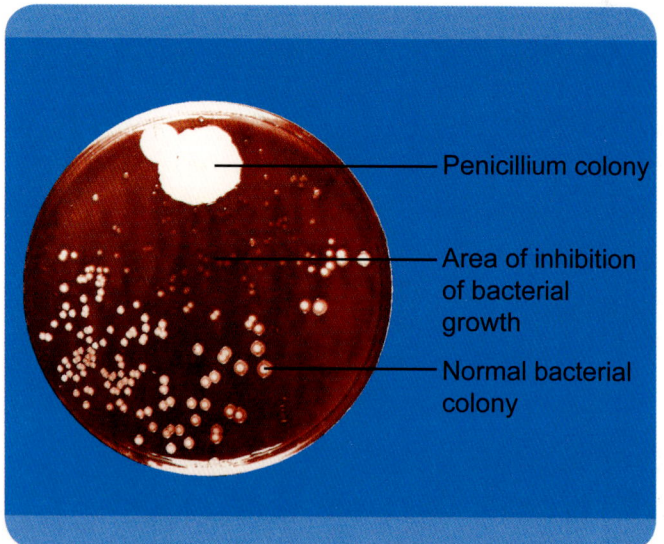

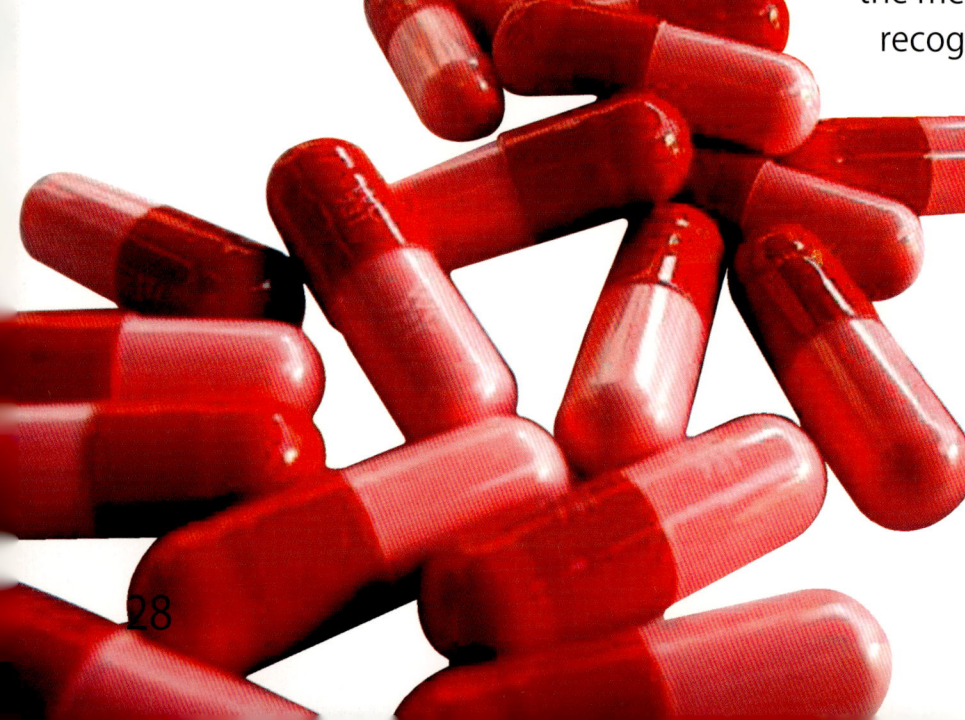

Penicillin was discovered accidentally by Dr. Alexander Fleming while working at St. Mary's Hospital in London. He was examining a culture of **Staphylococcus aureus**, a pathogenic bacterium when he noticed that it had been contaminated by a mold. He observed that species of the mold was inhibiting the bacterial growth. He took a sample of the mold and characterized it. He found that it belonged to penicillium family and could treat many types of harmful bacterial infections. Later, he named it penicillin and reported his findings in 1929. However, penicillin, the first antibiotic, was isolated by Howard Florey and Ernst Chain during the Second World War. This discovery revolutionized the medicinal research and recognized as the greatest advances in therapeutics. Fleming along with Florey and Chain received a Nobel Prize in 1945 for their discovery which led to the development of lifesaving antibiotics.

X-rays

Wilhelm Roentgen accidentally discovered X-rays when he was conducting experiments with the radiation from cathode rays. He noticed that the rays were able to penetrate opaque black paper wrapped around a cathode ray tube, causing a nearby table to glow with florescence. He also found that the new ray would pass through most substances casting shadows of solid objects on pieces of film. He named the new ray X-ray because in mathematics 'X' denotes the unknown quantity. The first image Roentgen took was an X-ray film of his wife Bertha's hand. The news of Roentgen's discovery spread quickly throughout the world. In early 1896, X-rays were being utilized clinically in the United States for capturing images of bone fractures and gunshot wounds. For this discovery, Roentgen was awarded with the first-ever Nobel Prize for physics in 1901.

Wilhelm Roentgen

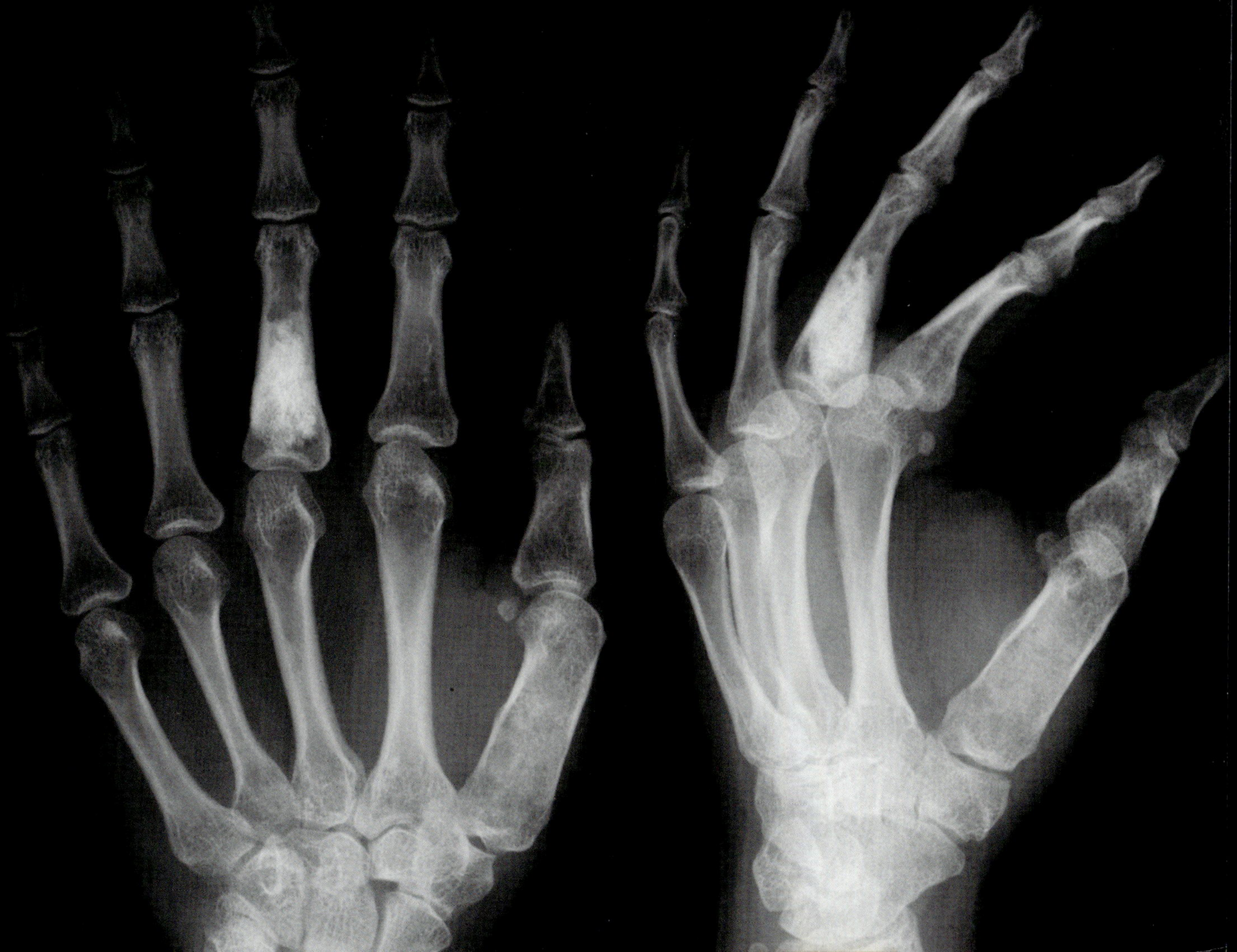

Human Immunodeficiency Virus (HIV)

Dr Montagnier and his colleagues discovered HIV as the cause **Human Immunodeficiency Virus**. Human Immunodeficiency Virus (HIV) is the causative agent of an infectious disease, **Acquired Immune Deficiency Syndrome** (AIDS). AIDS is a condition in humans in which the immune system begins to fail, leading to life-threatening opportunistic infections. Infection with HIV occurs by the transfer of blood, semen, vaginal fluid, pre-ejaculate or breast milk. Within these bodily fluids, HIV is present as both free virus particles and virus within infected immune cells. The four major routes of transmission are unsafe sex, contaminated needles, breast milk, and perinatal transmission (transmission from an infected mother to her baby at birth). AIDS was first recognized as a new disease in 1981, when a number of young men in New York and Los Angeles were diagnosed with symptoms not usually seen in individuals with healthy immune systems. This information was reported to the Centres for Disease Control and Prevention (CDC), the branch of the U.S. government that monitors and tries to control disease outbreaks.

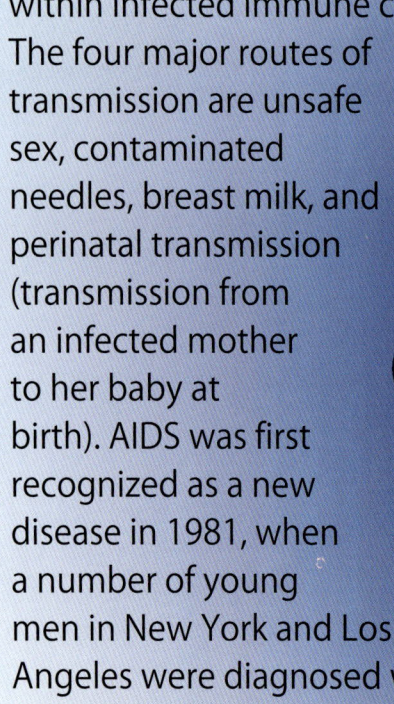
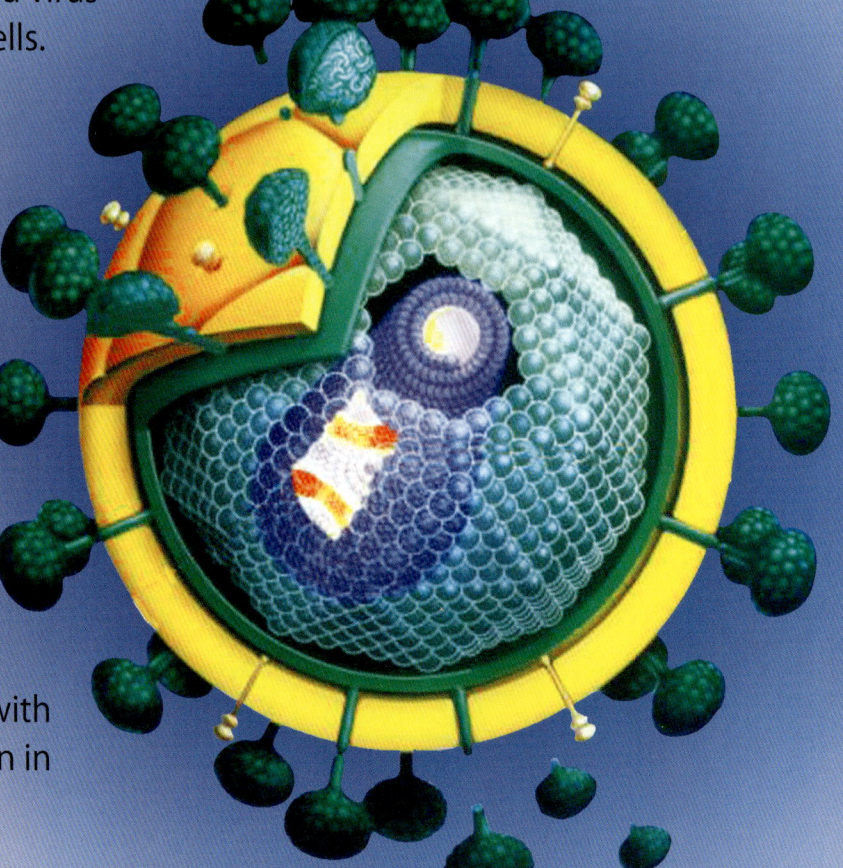

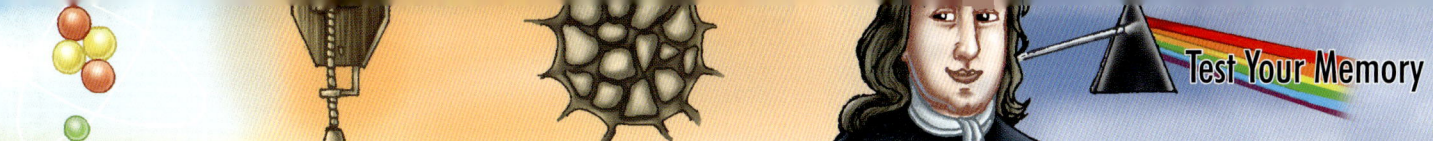

Test Your MEMORY

1. What is the difference between a discovery and an invention?

2. Who proposed the cell theory and what are the main postulates of this theory?

3. What is the big bang theory?

4. What is the Boyle's law of ideal gases?

5. What are the basic requirements of photosynthesis?

6. Explain Newton's laws of motion.

7. What is the universal law of gravitation?

8. Name the subatomic particles. Who discovered them?

9. Explain the law of conservation of mass.

10. What is anaesthesia used for?

11. What is HIV?

12. Describe the process of radioactive dating to find the age of a rock.

DISCOVERIES

Index

A
Acquired Immune Deficiency Syndrome 30
anaesthesia 15
antibiotic 28

B
barometer 3
beriberi 24
big bang theory 4

C
cathode ray 21, 29
cells 6, 7, 30
chlorophyll 11
combustion 12

D
dinosaurs 25
discoveries 3, 13

E
Earth 4, 12, 26
electron 20, 21
Ernest Marsden 22
Ernest Rutherford 22

F
force 9, 10
Frederick Gowland Hopkins 24

G
galaxies 4
Galileo 4, 14
glucose 11

H
haemophilia 27
Hans Geiger 22
Human Immunodeficiency Virus 30

I
inertia 9
inventions 3

J
James Chadwick 23
J.J. Thompson 21

M
magnetic field 21
marijuana 15
mass 9, 13, 19, 20, 21, 23

N
Neanderthal Man 8
neutron 20, 23
Nicolaus Copernicus 4
nucleus 6, 20, 22, 23
nutrients 11, 24

O
opium 15
oxygen 11, 12

P
penicillin 28
photosynthesis 11
pressure 3, 17
prism 18
proton 20, 22, 23

R
radiation 23, 29
radioactive dating 26
respiration 12
Rutherford-Bohr model 23

S
Staphylococcus aureus 28

T
transmission 30

V
vitamins 24
volume 17

W
William Fletcher 24

X
X-rays 29

PEGASUS ENCYCLOPEDIA LIBRARY

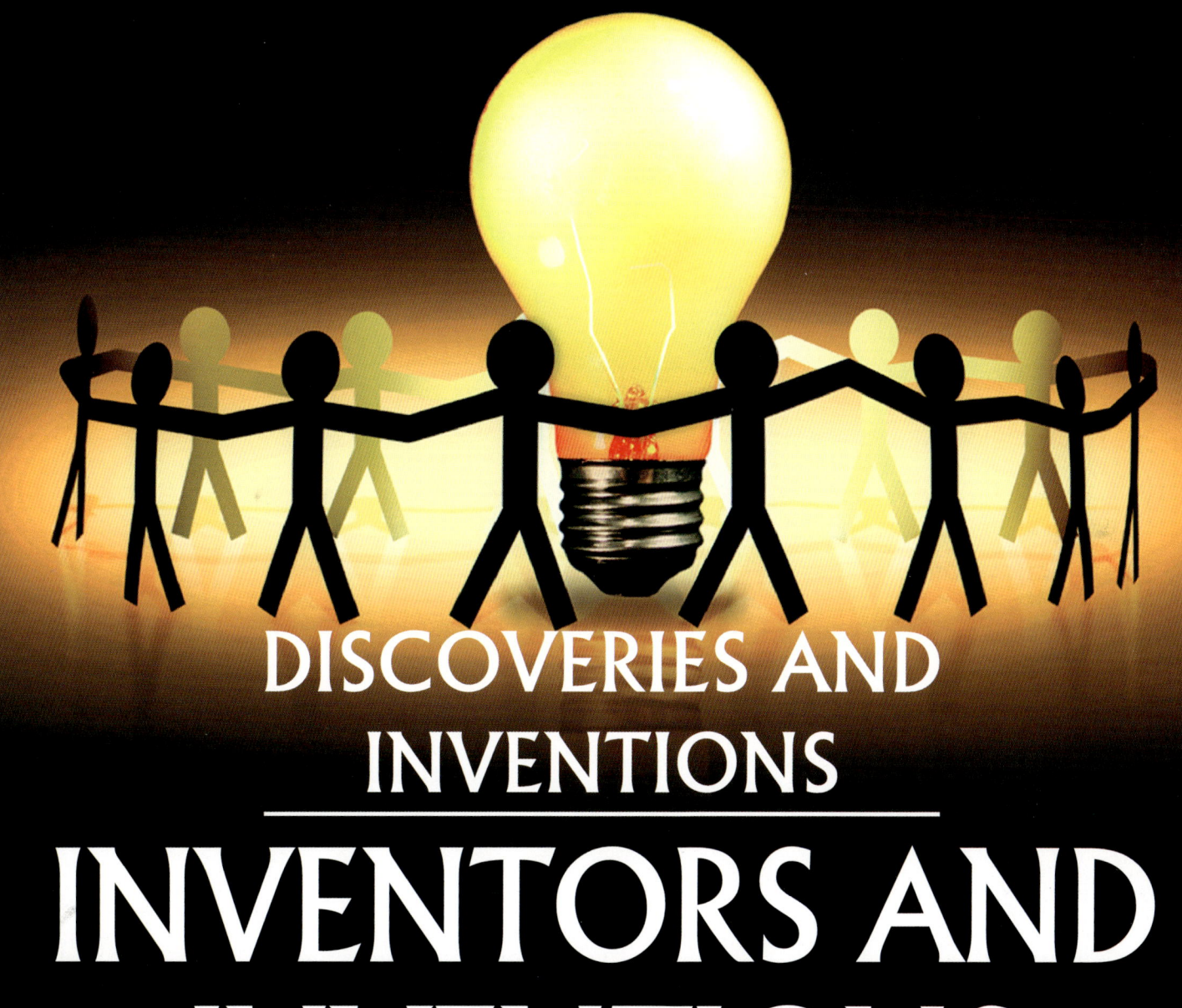

DISCOVERIES AND INVENTIONS

INVENTORS AND INVENTIONS

Edited by: Anil Kumar Tomar, Pallabi B. Tomar
Managing editor: Tapasi De
Designed by: Vijesh Chahal, Anil Kumar, Rohit Kumar
Illustrated by: Suman S. Roy, Tanoy Choudhury
Colouring done by: Vinay Kumar, Sonu, Kiran Kumari & Pradeep Kumar

INVENTORS AND INVENTIONS

CONTENTS

Inventions 3

- Compound microscope — 4
- Thermometer and Telescope — 5
- Adding machine — 6
- Barometer — 7
- Steam engine — 8
- Bifocal spectacles — 9
- Smallpox vaccination and Electric battery — 10
- Printing Press — 11
- Stethoscope and Galvanometer — 12
- Electric motor — 13
- Friction match — 14
- Typewriter — 15
- Braille printing and Sewing machine — 16
- Microphones and Television — 17
- Electric Lamp — 18
- Bicycle and Fountain pen — 19
- Telephone — 20
- Automobile engine — 21
- Kodak camera — 22
- Radio and Diesel engine — 23
- Aeroplane — 24
- Air conditioning — 25
- The guitar — 26
- Helicopter — 27
- Parachute — 28
- Blue Jeans and Electric Washing machine — 29
- Compact disc — 30

Test Your Memory 31

Index 32

Inventions

It has always been a great topic of debate whether scientific inventions are a boon or curse for us. No one can deny the fact that science and modern inventions have indeed been a blessing for mankind. We should always be grateful to scientists and inventors like Thomas Edison, James Watt and hundreds of other pioneers who carried out innumerable experiments with zeal and perseverance for the inventions of various gadgets and appliances that have made our life easier and entertaining. If science is a curse it is only because men with a criminal bent of mind misuse it for their own selfish ends.

This book lists some of the greatest inventions of all the times.

INVENTORS AND INVENTIONS

Anthony Van Leeuwenhoek

Compound microscope

A compound microscope is an instrument that uses combination of two or more lenses to produce magnified images of small objects. Zaccharias Hanssen invented the first microscope in 1590. He used several lenses in a tube and found that the object at the end of the tube was magnified significantly beyond the capability of a magnifying glass. This was the beginning of microscopy and he proposed that an image magnified by a single lens can be further magnified by a second lens. Anthony Van Leeuwenhoek took microscopy to higher levels and invented many microscopes with highly improved resolving power. He constructed more than 100 microscopes and is known as the father of microscopy. Leeuwenhoek and Robert Hooke are credited for the construction of microscopes for scientific purpose which marks the beginning of microbiology and cell biology.

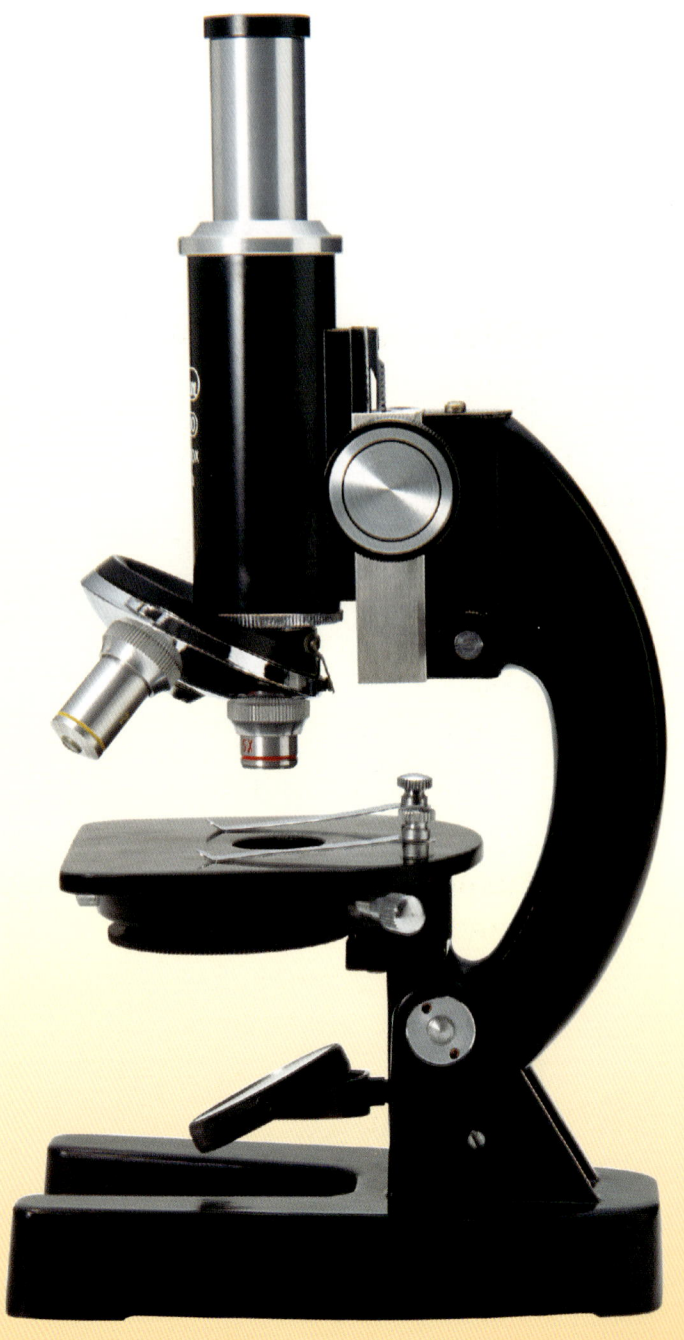

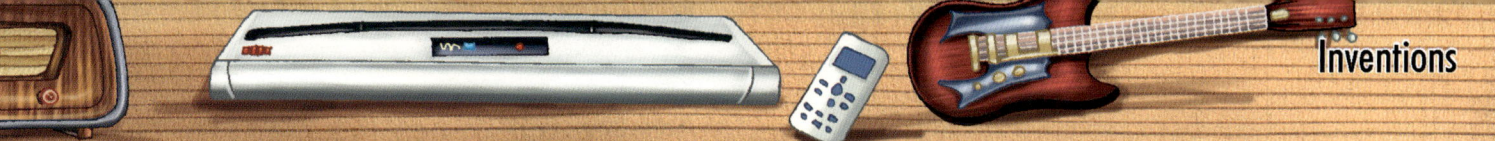

Inventions

Telescope

Telescope is defined as an optical instrument which is used for observing distant objects. This is made up by combination of mirrors or lenses which gather the visible light and make an object appear bigger and nearer for easy observation. In 1608, the first telescope was invented by a Dutch lens grinder, Hans Lippershey. Two other inventors, Zacharias Janssen and Jacob Metius are also credited for developing telescopes around the same time. Further improvements were made by Galileo Galilei who developed his own refractor telescope for astronomical studies in 1609. The British scientist Sir Isaac Newton constructed the first reflecting telescope using a concave primary mirror and a flat diagonal secondary mirror in the year 1668.

Isaac Newton

Galileo Galilei

Thermometer

Thermometer is an instrument that measures the temperature. The first thermometer was invented by an Italian, Santorio Santorio and it was called **thermoscope**. He was the first inventor to put a numerical scale on the temperature reading instrument. In 1593, Galileo Galilei invented a water thermometer. This thermometer for the first time allowed temperature variations to be measured. The modern mercury thermometer was invented by Gabriel Fahrenheit in 1714.

Astonishing fact

Charles Macintosh invented the waterproof coat, the Mackintosh, in 1823.

Telescope

INVENTORS AND INVENTIONS

Adding machine

In 1642, a French Mathematician and Physicist Blaise Pascal invented an adding machine. This machine used a train of 8 moveable dials to add or sum up to 8 numbers long and was capable of addition and subtraction only. This device was called Pascaline calculator which was the first digital calculating machine. The addition and subtraction were easy to perform on this calculator but multiplication and division procedures were quite complicated and inaccurate. In 1673, Gottfried Wilhelm Von Leibniz modified the **Pascaline calculator** and attached a multiplication/division device. Leibniz calculator was the first calculator capable of doing addition, subtraction, multiplication and division easily.

Astonishing fact

Music was sent down a telephone line for the first time in 1876, the year the phone was invented.

Inventions

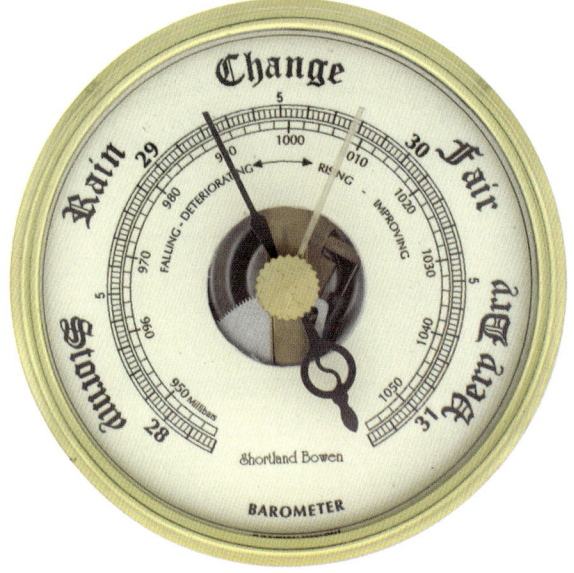

Evangelista Torricelli

Barometer

Barometer is a device which can measure atmospheric pressure or the weight of air in the atmosphere. In 1643, the first mercury barometer was invented by Evangelista Torricelli in Florence, Italy. In the basic device, an air less glass tube was inserted into a dish of mercury. The air pressing down on the mercury in the dish forced some of the mercury up into the glass tube. The rise in mercury levels was observed on the attached scale. In 1844, the first commercially viable aneroid barometer was made by Lucien Vidie in France. It consisted of an evacuated drum whose minute expansions and contractions under pressure changes could be measured by a needle moving over a dial.

7

INVENTORS AND INVENTIONS

Steam engine

A steam engine converts the potential energy that exists as pressure in steam and converts that to mechanical force. The steam locomotive trains that relied on steam engines for their movement marked the beginning of Industrial Revolution.

Denis Papin invented a digester or pressure cooker in the year 1679. Based on the theory of this invention an English engineer, Thomas Savery, designed the crude model of the first steam engine in 1698. The first commercial steam engine was built in the year 1712 by Thomas Newcomen. Though this invention got instant popularity and the engine was rugged and reliable but it had many faults resulting in wasted heat and fuel.

The first usable steam engine was patented by James Watt, a Scottish inventor in 1769. It had a separate condenser connected to a cylinder by a valve. This condenser kept the engine cool while cylinders were hot. Watt's engine is the basic design for all modern steam engines.

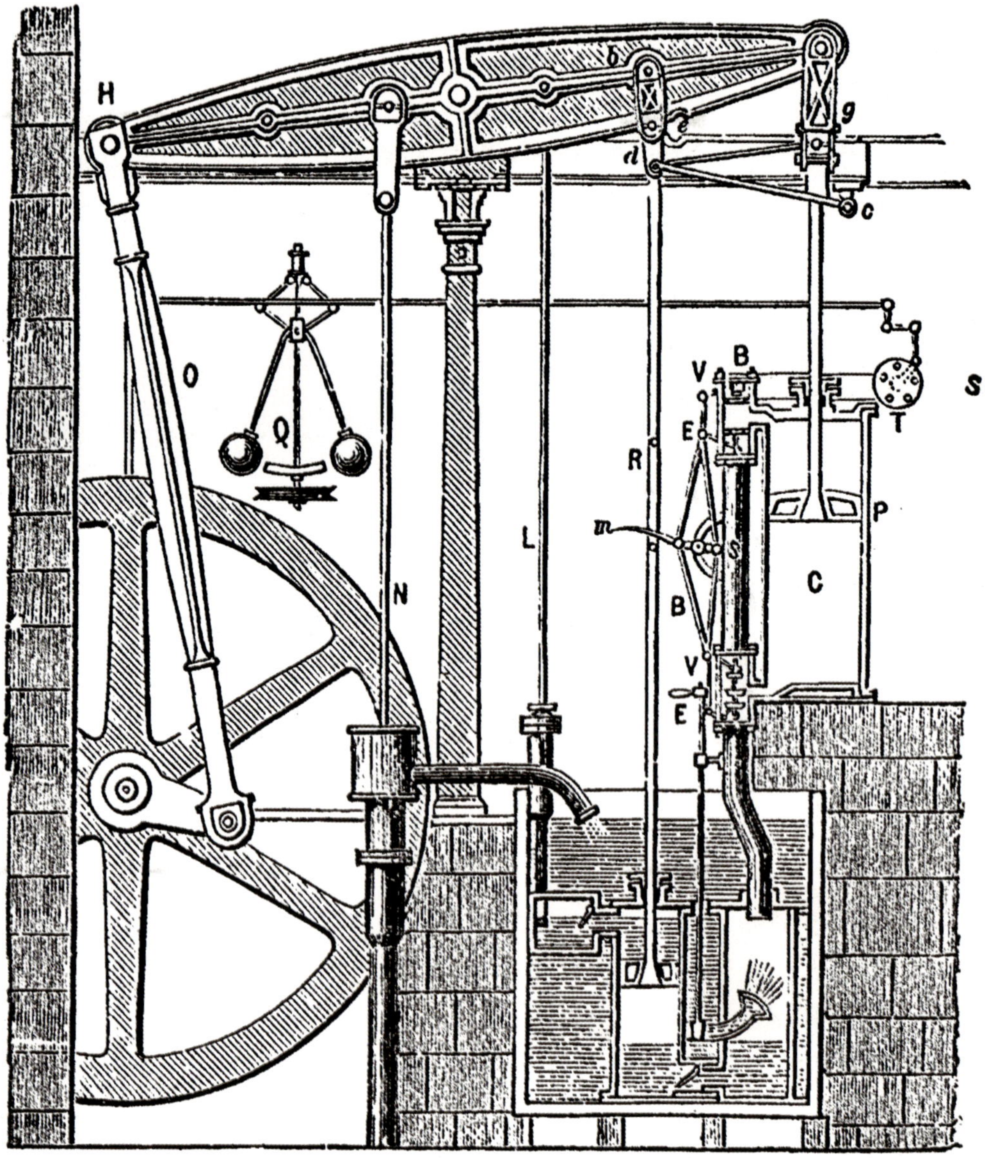

James Watt

Newcomen steam engine

8

Inventions

Bifocal spectacles

Bifocal spectacles are some of the most widely used glasses among people who have presbyopia and other near-sighted vision problems at the same time. Bifocal lens were invented by an American, Benjamin Franklin in 1780. Franklin was frustrated being both myopic (near-sighted) and hyperopic (far-sighted) because he had to constantly switch his pairs of glasses, depending on what he was trying to focus on. He longed for the ability to see both near and far with a single frame. In order to accomplish this, Benjamin had the lenses of two pairs of spectacles cut into half and put half of each lens in one sole frame. Today, millions of individuals take advantage of Franklin's bifocals which gives them a convenient way in which to correct their vision for both distance and reading.

Benjamin Franklin

Least convex for distant objects

Most convex for reading

Least convex

Most convex

INVENTORS AND INVENTIONS

Smallpox vaccination

Edward Jenner

For many centuries, smallpox devastated mankind. In modern times we do not have to worry about it. Thanks to the remarkable work of Edward Jenner and the later developments from his endeavours. In 1796, he invented the smallpox vaccination. Dr Jenner was aware of the belief that people who contracted cowpox, never contracted smallpox. He realized that inoculating people with cowpox would immunize them against smallpox. He researched this issue and performed a test to confirm his hypothesis. He inoculated an eight-year-old boy, Phipps, with matter taken from a cowpox pustule. The matter was taken from the hand of Sarah Nelmes, who had caught the disease from a cow named Blossom. Phipps developed coxpox and quickly recovered. Several weeks later, the boy was inoculated with smallpox and he did not contract the disease.

Electric battery

Volta battery

In 1800, after extensive experimentation, an Italian physicist Alessandro Volta developed the voltaic pile or electric battery. The original voltaic pile consisted of a pile of zinc and silver discs and between alternate discs a piece of cardboard was soaked in saltwater. A wire connecting the bottom zinc disc to the top silver disc could produce repeated sparks.

Inventions

Printing press

In 1803, Frederick Koenig produced the Suhl press which was basically a powered, wooden hand press with moveable carriage, reciprocating platen, self-opening frisket and self-inking 'cylinders'. These cylinders were wooden rollers wrapped with layers of felt and covered with leather. This machine was considered too complicated and costly by German printers. Later, Koenig was joined by his fellow countryman and good friend, Andreas F. Bauer. Bauer was a mechanic or watchmaker by profession. Together they combined their ideas and constructed the first actual printing machine powered by steam in 1810.

Frederick Koenig

Astonishing fact

The videophone was invented by Bell Laboratories in 1927.

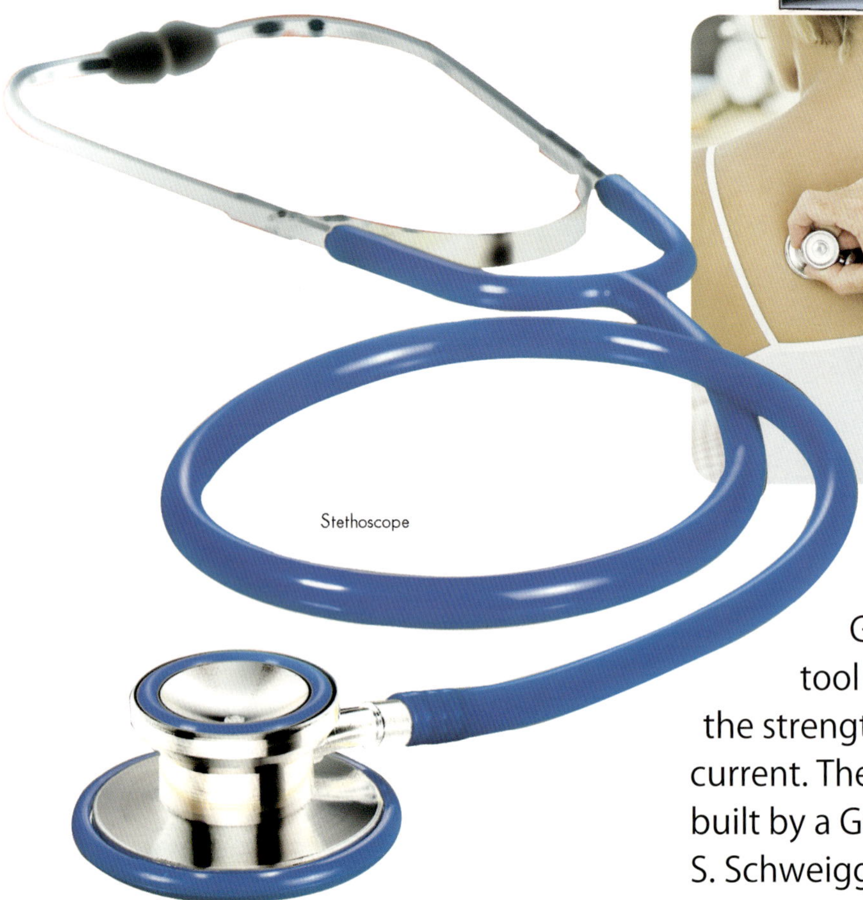

INVENTORS AND INVENTIONS

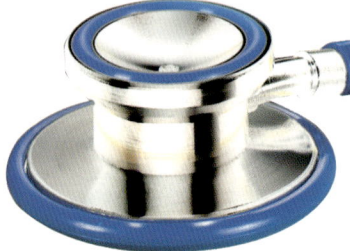
Stethoscope

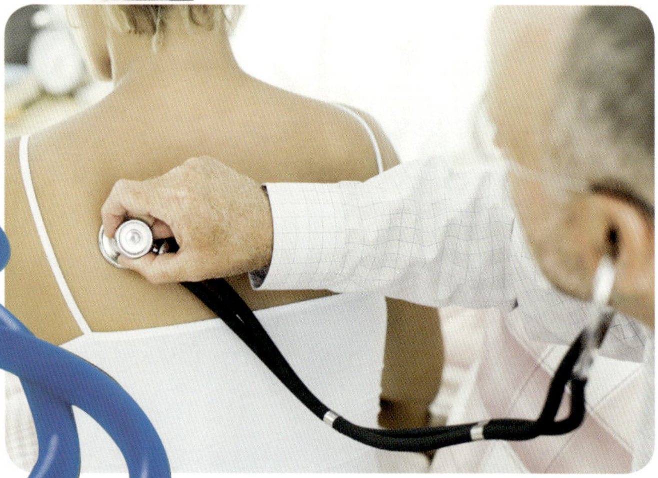

Galvanometer

Galvanometer is an electronic tool which is used for measuring the strength and direction of electric current. The first galvanometer was built by a German inventor, Johann S. Schweigger in 1820. It was the first sensitive instrument for measuring and detecting small amounts of electricity.

Stethoscope

The stethoscope is a common instrument to all doctors which is used for auscultation, or listening to the internal sounds of an animal body or a human body. Rene Theophile Hyacinthe Laennec, a French physician, invented the stethoscope in 1819. Using this new instrument, he investigated the sounds made by the heart and lungs and determined that his diagnoses were supported by the observations made during autopsies. The word stethoscope comes from the Greek words 'stethos' meaning chest and 'skopein' meaning to explore.

Galvanometer

Inventions

Electric motor

British physicist and chemist, Michael Faraday is best known for his discoveries of electromagnetic induction and of the laws of electrolysis. His biggest breakthrough in electricity was his invention of the electric motor in the year 1821. Electric motors transform electrical energy into mechanical energy. Michael Faraday built two devices to produce what he called electromagnetic rotation; that is a continuous circular motion from the circular magnetic force around a wire. He also proved that if mechanical energy was sent back through an electric motor it is transformed into electricity. The electrical generators are based on this principle. He also discovered electromagnetic induction. His experiments formed the basis of modern electromagnetic technology.

Michael Faraday

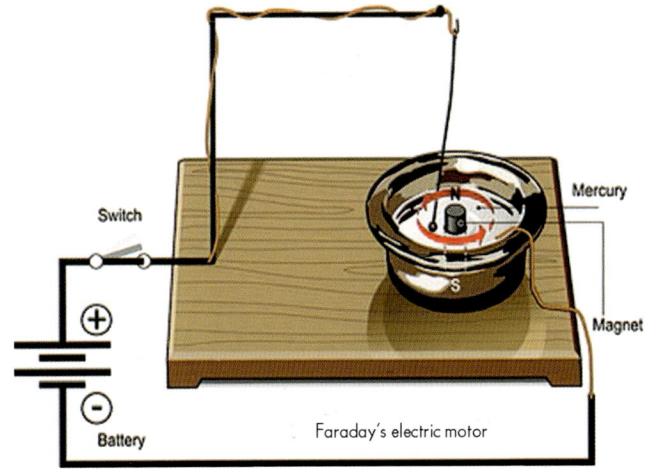

Faraday's electric motor

Astonishing fact

The first vending machine was invented by Hero of Alexandria in the first century. When a coin was dropped into a slot, its weight would pull a cork out of a spigot and the machine would dispense a trickle of holy water.

INVENTORS AND INVENTIONS

Friction match

In 1826, John Walker, a chemist in Stockton, accidently discovered that a stick coated with chemicals burst into flame when scraped across his hearth at home. This gave him the idea to invent the first friction match. Walker's friction match revolutionised the production, application and the portability of the fire. Walker sold his first 'Friction Light' in 1827 from his pharmacy. Initially, his friction matches were made of cardboard but he soon began to use wooden splints cut by hand. Later on, he packaged the matches in a cardboard box equipped with a piece of sandpaper for striking. Samuel Jones of London copied Walker's idea and launched his own 'Lucifers' (an early type of friction match) in 1829 which were an exact copy of Walker's friction lights.

Astonishing fact

The Monopoly game was invented by Charles Darrow in 1933. He sold the rights to George Parker in 1935. Parker invented more than 100 games, including Pit, Rook, Flinch, Risk and Clue.

John Walker

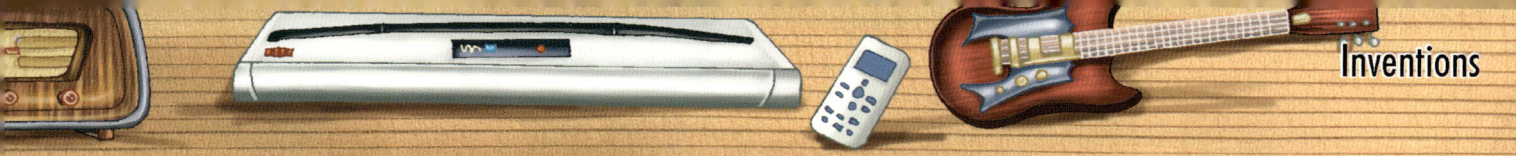

Inventions

Typewriter

In pre computer days, the typewriter was the most significant everyday business tool for typing the texts. In 1829, William Austin Burt invented the typographer, the predecessor of the typewriter. Christopher Latham Sholes, a U.S. mechanical engineer, invented the first practical modern typewriter in 1868. Sholes invented the commercial typewriter with partners S. W. Soule and G. Glidden that was manufactured by Remington Arms Company in 1873. This typewriter was the first device that allowed an operator to type substantially faster than a person could write by hand. The action of the type bars in the early typewriters was very sluggish and tended

Christopher Latham Sholes

to jam frequently. To fix this problem, Sholes obtained a list of the most common letters used in English, and rearranged the keyboard of the typewriter from an alphabetic arrangement to one in which the most common pairs of letters were spread fairly far apart on the keyboard.

INVENTORS AND INVENTIONS

Braille printing

Braille printing is a system of raised dots that is read with the fingers as they are embossed on paper. In 1829 a blindman of France, Louis Braille developed an ingenious system of reading and writing for blinds by means of raised dots. He was accidentally blinded in his childhood. Today, in virtually every language throughout the world, Braille is the standard form of writing and reading used by visually impaired persons.

Sewing machine

Sewing machine is used to stitch fabric, cards and other materials together with the thread. It is believed that the first known attempt for a workable sewing machine was framed in 1790 by Thomas Saint. In 1830, Barthelemy Thimonnier, a French tailor, invented the first functional sewing machine. It used only one thread and a hooked needle for a chain stitch. In 1834, Walter Hunt invented the double-thread sewing machine and it was regarded as America's first successful sewing machine. The machine devised by Walter Hunt was a straight-seam sewing machine which used a reciprocating eye-pointed needle and an oscillating shuttle.

Inventions

Microphones

A microphone is an instrument for intensifying weak sounds. It detects sound signals and transforms sound waves into electrical impulses. Sir Charles Wheatstone in 1827 was the first person to use the word 'microphone'. In 1876, Emile Berliner invented the first microphone which was used as a voice transmitter. David Edward Hughes invented the advanced carbon microphone in 1878. These microphones became common with more technical developments during the 1920s. The broadcasting microphones were developed after the invention of the radio.

Television

Today, the television has become a common source of entertainment in all households. It is a medium of telecommunication for transmitting and receiving moving images accompanied by sound. John Logie Baird, in 1925, invented the television. He was the first man to demonstrate the moving images in London. Philo Farnsworth, an American inventor, is accredited with the invention of the first fully electronic television system. He televised a motion picture on September 1, 1928.

INVENTORS AND INVENTIONS

Electric lamp

In 1800, Humphrey Davy connected wires to an electric battery and a piece of carbon. He observed that carbon glowed and produced light. This was the first electric light invented and he called it 'carbon electric arc'. Sir Joseph Wilson Swan devised an idea for practical, long-lasting electric light. He experimented with carbon paper filaments but these filaments burnt up quickly. Thomas Alva Edison experimented with thousands of different filaments to find just the right materials to glow well and be long-lasting. Edison discovered that a carbon filament in an oxygen-free bulb glowed but did not burn up for long time. In 1879, he improved upon all previous designs to produce the first reliable, commercial electric light bulb. The basic design was a sealed, evacuated glass bulb containing a filament connected by wires to an outside source of electric current.

Thomas Alva Edison

Astonishing fact

The first fax process was invented in 1843.

Inventions

Bicycle

Kirkpatrick Macmillan was born in Coathill, Scotland, in 1812. The idea of inventing a bicycle came to his mind when he saw someone on a velocipede, a two wheeled frame that was pushed along by the rider's feet. He decided to build one for himself and when it was completed, he thought that it would be a huge improvement if he could propel it without putting his feet on the ground. He worked hard on his imagination and made many improvements in the basic velocipede. Finally, in 1838, he completed the world's first ever pedal bicycle. The pedals were attached to rods, which directly connected to the hub of the rear wheel. He was a countryman and had no interest in patenting his invention.

Fountain pen

In 1883, Lewis Edson Waterman, an American insurance salesman, invented the first practical fountain pen. The pen held its own ink supply and used capillary action to control the ink flow. There had been hundreds of patent claims for fountain pens before Waterman filed one in the year 1884, but Waterman's patent was the only reliable work. He had almost spent ten years perfecting his invention. He established the Waterman Fountain Pen Company in the same year. Initially, all his pens were handmade and he sold them through his brother's cigar shop. Waterman also invented a process for condensing and preserving grape juice.

Lewis Edson Waterman

INVENTORS AND INVENTIONS

Alexander Graham Bell

Telephone

Telephone is one of the biggest invention in the field of communication. In pre-telephone era, the one could only speak to someone who stood face to face. In 1836, electric telegraph was invented by William Cooke and Charles Wheatstone for long distance communications. They developed the first electric telegraph for commercial services in England in 1838. The telegraph lines used visual signals to relay messages from one elevated location to the next. In 1876 the Scotsman, Alexander Graham Bell demonstrated a piece of equipment that allowed people to speak to each other over great distances. He called his invention— the telephone.

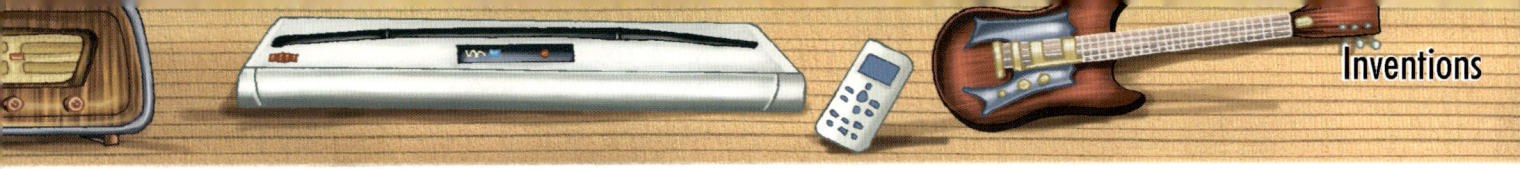

Inventions

Astonishing fact

During the 1860s, George Leclanche developed the dry-cell battery, the basis for modern batteries.

Automobile engine

In 1885, German mechanical engineer, Karl Benz designed and built the world's first usable automobile to be powered by an internal-combustion engine. He received the first patent for a gas-fueled car in 1886. The car was three wheeled and had an electric ignition, differential gears and water-cooling. He built his first four wheeler car in 1891 and founded the automobile company, Benz & Company. The company became the world's largest manufacturer of automobiles by 1900.

INVENTORS AND INVENTIONS

Kodak camera

In early days of photography, photographers had to coat a plate with wet chemical each time they wanted to take a picture. The process was called the **Collodion process** and was a very discouraging process. In 1880, George Eastman modified the process for making gelatin dry plates which was invented in 1971 by Richard Maddox for photography. The increased speed and sensitivity to light of the dryplates freed the camera from the tripod and cemented the way for the handheld camera, an instrument for instant photography at very low cost.

In 1881, George Eastman founded the Eastman Kodak Company. He invented the roll paper film in 1885 and celluloid film in 1889 which brought photography to everybody. The roll film was also the basis of the invention of the motion picture film, used by early filmmakers. In the year 1888, Eastman registered the trademark Kodak and received a patent for his handheld camera. The handheld camera used a roll film containing a 100 exposure paper stripping film.

Astonishing fact

In 1894 Thomas Edison and W K L Dickson introduced the first film camera.

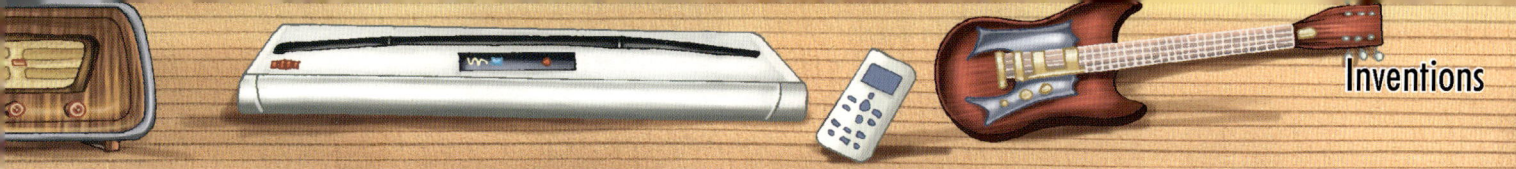

Inventions

Radio

Guglielmo Marconi was fascinated by Heinrich Hertz's discovery of radio waves and realized that it can be used for sending and receiving telegraph messages. In 1896, he sent the first radio signals over a telephone. These transmissions were coded signals that were transmitted only about a kilometer far. He referred them as 'wireless telegraphs'. He established the first radio link between Britain and France in 1899. In 1909 Marconi shared the Nobel prize in physics for his wireless telegraph. Marconi introduced short wave transmission in 1922 that marked the transmission of voice over the air or the birth of the modern radio.

The engine developed by Nikolaus Otto used a spark plug to ignite the fuel. In 1892, Rudolf Diesel developed the idea of eliminating the spark plug from an engine. In 1893, he successfully built the first internal combustion engine. His engine relied on a high compression of the fuel to ignite it.

Diesel engine

A **diesel engine** is an internal combustion engine. It uses the heat of compression to initiate ignition to burn the fuel. The fuel is injected into the combustion chamber during the final stage of compression.

Diesel engine

23

INVENTORS AND INVENTIONS

Aeroplane

For many years the scientific researchers through out the world were engaged in designing and inventing an aeroplane. Many unsuccessful attempts were made in the 19th century. In 1903, Wilbur Wright and his younger brother, Orville Wright invented the first aeroplane. Around 1896, the Wright brothers read the newspapers stories about the invention of gliders and the inventors who were trying to fly. This triggered the imagination of both brothers to build an aircraft. They analysed the available information on flight experiments and found that all the aircrafts developed till then, lacked controls. They tried various improvements in the previous designs and started building their aircrafts. They decided to use Kitty Hawk, North Carolina to test the various models they had built. In 1900 and 1901, they launched two gliders but were disappointed with the performance due to lack of lift and control. Towards the end of 1902, they launched their third glider with roll, pitch and yaw controls. They also designed the first ever aeroplane propellers and finally built a new, powered aircraft. After many unsuccessful attempts, the Wright brothers made aeronautical history in the last month of the year 1903 when Orville Wright took the first flight in their aircraft for 12 seconds covering 120 ft! In the next few hours the brothers made 4 flights and the longest flight was of 852 ft. This was the first successful airplane invented by the Wright brothers.

Air conditioning

The development of refrigeration started in the early days with the need to preserve foods. Foods that are kept at room temperature spoil easily due to contamination by microbes such as bacteria. The principles of the absorption type of refrigeration was discovered as early as 1824 and showed that liquified ammonia could chill air when it is allowed to evaporate. In 1842, a physician John Gorrie created ice using compressor technology. The first electrical air conditioning was invented by an American, Willis Haviland Carrier in the year 1902. For his achievements in the field of air conditioning, he is known as the Father of Modern Air Conditioning. In the beginning, the commercially available air conditioning applications were manufactured for the need to cool air for industrial processes. The devices were restricted to industrial purposes and could not find place to be used for personal comfort. The main reason was that refrigerant gases used in initial applications such as ammonia were toxic and flammable. In 1928, Thomas Midgley, Jr., discovered Freon as a safer refrigerant to humans. This marked the beginning of the air conditioning systems for all residential, industrial and commercial applications.

INVENTORS AND INVENTIONS

The guitar

The guitar is a musical instrument having a flat-backed rounded body that narrows in the middle, a long fretted neck, and which is played by strumming or plucking. The guitar is a European invention that first appeared during the medieval period. The invention of modern classical guitar is credited to Antonio Torres circa, a Spanish guitar maker. He made the first modern guitar in the year 1850. He increased the size of the guitar body, altered its proportions and invented the top bracing pattern. These modifications greatly improved the volume, tone and projection of the instrument. In 1931, George Beauchamp and Adolph Rickenbacker introduced the first commercially viable, electric guitar. It was known as the 'Frying Pan'.

Astonishing fact

The first neon sign was made in 1923 for a Packard dealership.

Helicopter

Although, Europeans had invented the helicopter but Igor Ivanovich Sikorsky, an American, was the first man to put a true helicopter into full production. The internal combustion engine made it possible for the pioneers to develop full-sized models of an aircraft with an adequate power source. However, there were many problems that had not been worked out on any one individual helicopter. In 1907, the French pioneer Paul Cornu invented the first helicopter. He lifted a twin-rotored helicopter into the air entirely without assistance from the ground for a few seconds. This invention marked the beginning of history of helicopters. Several models were produced by many designs afterwards but there were no more great advances until another French, Etienne Oehmichen, became the first to fly a helicopter a kilometer in a closed circuit in 1924. It was a historic flight which took 7 minutes and 40 seconds. Igor Sikorsky invented the first successful helicopter in 1939 upon which further designs were based. His helicopter had the control to fly safely forwards and backwards, up and down, and sideways. For his achievement, he is called the 'father' of helicopters. By 1940, his helicopter VS-300 had become the model for all modern single-rotor helicopters. He also designed and built the first military helicopter, XR-4. In 1958, his rotorcraft company made the world's first helicopter that had a boat hull and could land and takeoff from water. It could also float on the water.

INVENTORS AND INVENTIONS

Parachute

A parachute is a device for slowing down the speed of a falling body in the atmosphere by creating a drag. The first parachute was imagined and sketched centuries ago by Leonardo da Vinci. Sebastien Lenormand is credited for the invention of first practical parachute. He demonstrated the principle of a parachute in 1783. Andrew Garnerin in 1797, was the first man to jump with a parachute without a rigid frame. Garnerin designed the first air vent in a parachute intended to reduce oscillations. In 1890, Paul Letteman and Kathchen Paulus invented the method of folding or packing the parachute in a knapsack to be worn on the back before its release. Paulus also invented the advanced parachutes in which one small parachute opens first and pulls open the main parachute. Two parachutters, Grant Morton and Captain Albert Berry, made the first parachuted jump from an airplane in 1911.

Astonishing fact

The hair perm was invented in 1906 by Karl Ludwig Nessler of Germany.

Inventions

Blue jeans

Levi Strauss is credited for the invention of denim or blue jeans. Levi Strauss & Company was founded by him in the year 1853. Initially, he started selling rough canvas pants to the gold mine workers. These pants were very strong but they tended to chafe. After a few complaints, Strauss substituted the canvas with a twilled cotton fabric from France called 'serge de Nimes'. The fabric eventually became known as 'denim' and the pants were nicknamed 'blue jeans'. In 1860, Strauss strengthened the pockets of his trousers with copper rivets. In 1873, he partnered with Jacob Davis, a tailor in Reno, Nevada, and started making men's work pants with metal rivets for strength.

Electric washing machine

Ancient peoples cleaned their clothes by pounding them on rocks or rubbing them with abrasive sands and washing the dirt away in local streams. James King, an American, built the first washing machine using a drum in 1851, resembling a modern machine. But this machine was hand powered. The first electric-powered washing machine was invented by Alva J. Fisher in 1908. It was introduced and marketed by the Hurley Machine Company of Chicago, Illinois.

INVENTORS AND INVENTIONS

Compact disc

A compact disc or CD, is an optical storage medium with digital data recorded on it. The digital data can be in the form of audio, video or computer information. When the CD is played, the information is read or detected by a tightly focused light source called a laser beam. In 1965, the first compact disc was manufactured by James Russell. Russell was granted with more than 20 patents for various elements of compact disc system. Electronic Manufacturers Sony and Philips are credited for developing the compact disc in 1981. The compact disc gained popularity only after these companies started manufacturing CDs for commercial purpose.

Test Your MEMORY

1. Who is known as the father of microscopy?
2. What is the difference between a microscope and a telescope?
3. Write a short note on Pascaline Calculator.
4. When was the barometer invented? What was the basic set up of first barometer?
5. What is a steam engine?
6. Why do we use bifocal lenses?
7. What is a stethoscope?
8. Who was Michael Faraday?
9. Write a short history of typewriters.
10. Give an account of the invention of the bicycle.
11. When was the first aeroplane invented?
12. What is a compact disc?

Index

A
adding machine 6
aeroplane 24
aeroplane propellers 24
aneroid barometer 7
atmospheric pressure 7

B
bacteria 25
bicycle 19
bifocal spectacles 9
braille printing 16

C
carbon electric arc 18
carbon filament 18
cell biology 4
celluloid film 22
collodion process 22
compact disc 30
compound microscope 4

D
denim 29
diesel engine 23
digester 8
digital data 30

E
electric light bulb 18
electric motor 13
electric telegraph 20
electromagnetic induction 13

G
galvanometer 12
gelatin dry plates 22

H
helicopter 27
hyperopic 9

I
industrial revolution 8
internal combustion engine 23, 27

K
keyboard 15

L
laws of electrolysis 13
lenses 4, 5, 9
liquified ammonia 25

M
magnifying glass 4
mercury barometer 7
microbiology 4
microphone 17
microscopy 4

P
pascaline calculator 6
presbyopia 9
printing press 11

R
radio waves 23
refrigeration 25

S
smallpox 10
sound waves 17
steam engine 8
suhl press 11

T
telescope 5
thermometer 5
thermoscope 5

V
vaccination 10
velocipede 19

W
washing machine 29
water thermometer 5
wireless telegraphs 23

PEGASUS ENCYCLOPEDIA LIBRARY

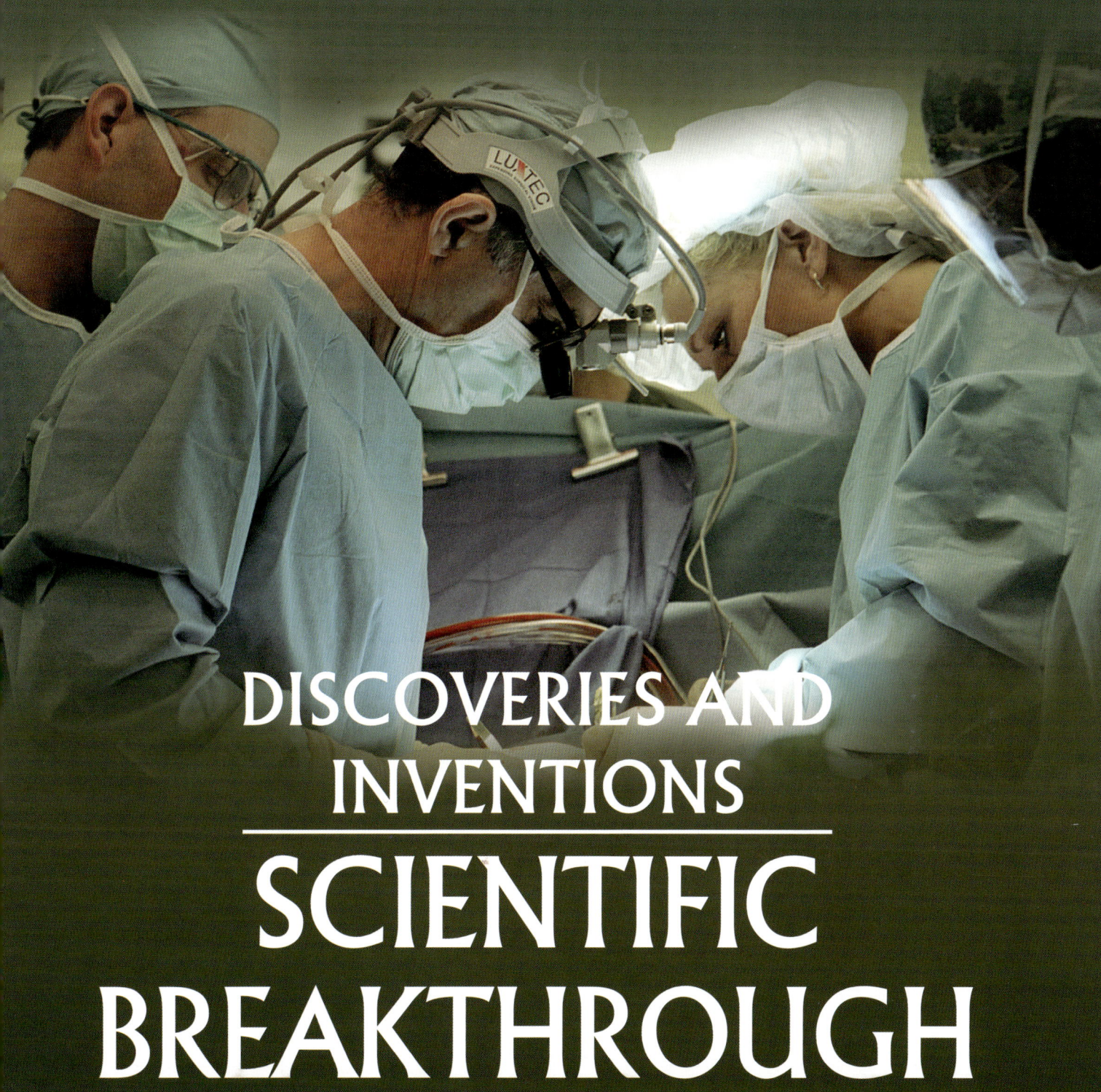

DISCOVERIES AND INVENTIONS
SCIENTIFIC BREAKTHROUGH

Edited by: Anil Kumar Tomar, Pallabi B. Tomar
Managing editor: Tapasi De
Designed by: Vijesh Chahal, Anil Kumar, Rohit Kumar
Illustrated by: Suman S. Roy, Tanoy Choudhury
Colouring done by: Vinay Kumar, Sonu, Kiran Kumari & Pradeep Kumar

SCIENTIFIC BREAKTHROUGH

CONTENTS

The first heart transplant 3
The first lunar landing 4
The first man on moon 5
The first space satellite 6
The first photograph 8
Evolution of photography and its elements 9
The first test tube baby 13
First cloned animal 14
The first computer 15
The first computer mouse 16
The first motorcycle 17
The first X-Ray 18
The first microprocessor 19
Aspirin— the miracle drug 20
Penicillin—the first antibiotic 22
ARPANET—the beginning of internet 23
Water purification 24
Robot 26
Artificial limb 27
The first vaccine—Smallpox vaccination 28
Open-heart surgery 29
The human genome 30
Test Your Memory 31
Index 32

The first heart transplant

South African cardiac surgeon, Dr Christiaan Barnard, is famous for performing the world's first successful human heart transplant.

Barnard was born on November 8, 1922, in Beaufort West, South Africa, son of a minister in Reformed Church. One of his brothers died of a heart problem while a toddler— an event which affected the Barnard family seriously.

Barnard studied at the University of Cape Town Medical School, did his internship and residency at the Groote Schuur Hospital in Cape Town and became a general practitioner in Ceres, in Western Cape province.

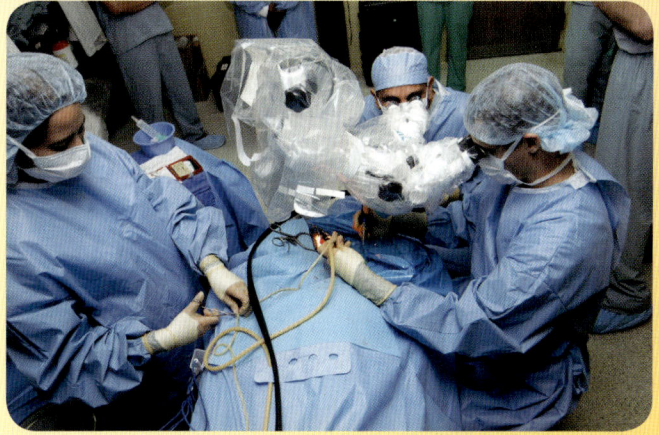

Barnard performed the world's first human heart transplant operation on 3 December, 1967 assisted by his brother, Marius Barnard, lasting nine hours and using a team of 30 persons.

The patient, Louis Washkansky was 55 years old and suffering from diabetes and heart disease. The transplant heart came from a young woman, Denise Darvall, killed in a road accident. Washkansky survived the operation and lived for 18 days, succumbing to pneumonia induced by the immuno-suppressive drugs he was taking.

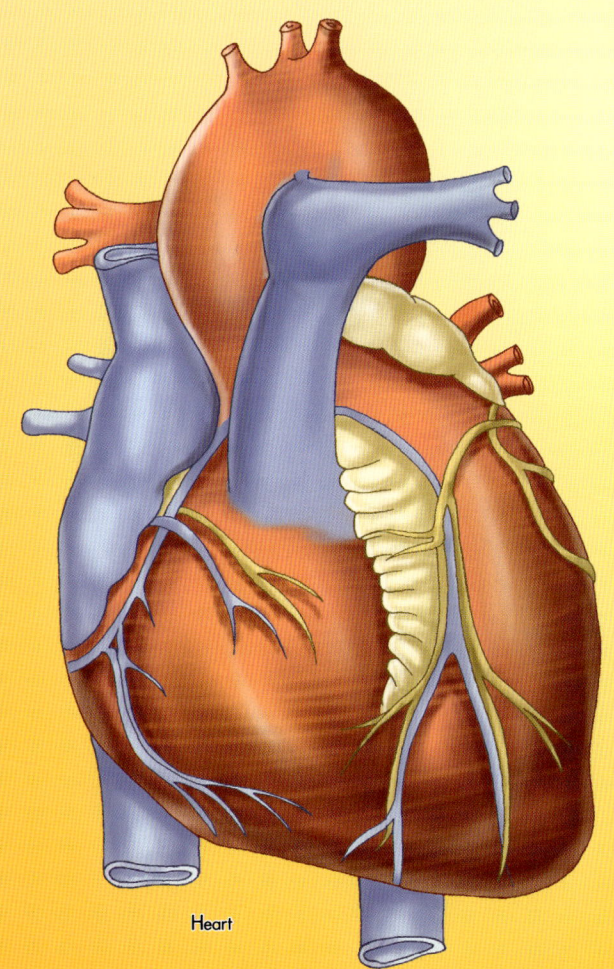

Heart

The first truly synthetic plastic was invented by Leo Baekeland, a Belgium chemist living in New York.

SCIENTIFIC BREAKTHROUGH

The first lunar landing

The first object from Earth to ever land on the Moon was the Soviet spacecraft Luna-2. It didn't land, but actually crashed into the Moon on September 14, 1959. It impacted the lunar surface west of Mare Serenitatis near the craters Aristides, Archimedes and Autolycus of the moon. Luna 2's mission was to help confirm the discovery of the solar wind turned up by Luna 1.

The first US spacecraft to impact the Moon was Ranger 7, which crashed into the Moon on July 31, 1964. This came after a string of failures with previous spacecraft in the Pioneer and Ranger line of robotic spacecraft.

The first spacecraft to make a soft landing on the Moon was the Soviet Luna-9 on February 3, 1966. Luna-9 was equipped with an airbag system that allowed it to crash into the Moon travelling more than 50 km/hour. The first even softer landing was made by US with Surveyor 1. It touched down on the surface of the Moon on June 2, 1966.

The first man on the moon

The 1st man on the moon was the Apollo 11 Commander Neil Armstrong, who made history on July 20, 1969.

The Apollo 11 mission consisted of Command Module Pilot Michael Collins, Lunar Module Pilot Buzz Aldrin and Commander Neil Armstrong. The mission launched atop a Saturn V rocket on July 16, 1969. After a 4 day journey from the Earth to the Moon, the lunar module detached from the command module and landed on the surface of the Moon in the southern Sea of Tranquility.

The crew remained inside the module for 6 and half hours, preparing to make their exit onto the lunar surface. And then Neil Armstrong descended the ladder from the lunar module and onto the lunar surface. Buzz Aldrin followed Armstrong, and the two remained on the surface of the Moon for 2.5 hours, taking photographs, collecting rocks, drilling samples and placing scientific experiments. They gathered up all their samples, packed them in the lunar module, and left some souvenirs on the surface of the Moon like an American flag, Apollo 1 mission patch and commemorative plaque. They launched again and returned to Earth on July 24.

SCIENTIFIC BREAKTHROUGH

Robert Hutchings Goddard was an American physicist and inventor who is known as the father of modern rocketry.

The first space satellite

The space age began with the October 4, 1957 launch of the first Russian space satellite. Other Sputnik satellites and the first US Explorer satellite soon followed.

Sputnik 1

The space age began with the October 4, 1957 launch of the first artificial space satellite, Sputnik 1. The name Sputnik comes from Russian for 'companion' or 'fellow traveller'.

Sputnik 1 was a very simple satellite. It was a highly polished aluminum sphere. Sputnik 1 was 22 inches in diameter and weighed 183 pounds. Radio antennas extended from the sphere.

The first Sputnik's only instrumentation was a battery powered radio transmitter and a thermometer. Sputnik sent radio telemetry back to Earth. It orbited Earth every 98 minutes and fell back to Earth on January 4, 1958. The importance of this first Sputnik was not the data or telemetry but the simple fact that a manmade object had been launched into the orbit!

The first space satellite

Sputnik 2

When they realized the impact of the first Sputnik, Soviet leaders asked for a larger satellite launch in time to celebrate the 40th anniversary of the Russian revolution. Sputnik 2 was designed and built very quickly. It launched less than a month later on November 3, 1957.

Sputnik 2 was considerably larger. The 1,120 pound satellite carried the first passenger into space. A dog Laika, travelled into space but soon died when the capsule overheated. The satellite however remained in the orbit a little over 6 months.

Sputnik 3

The first attempt to launch Sputnik 3 on April 27, 1958 failed. Sputnik 3 was however successfully launched on May 15, 1958. The 1.5 ton satellite contained a scientific payload with scientific instruments for measuring the conditions in space.

> In the 1980s, Luc Montagnier and Robert Gallo both separately discovered the retro virus known as HIV (Human Immunodeficiency Virus). This was also identified as the cause of AIDS.

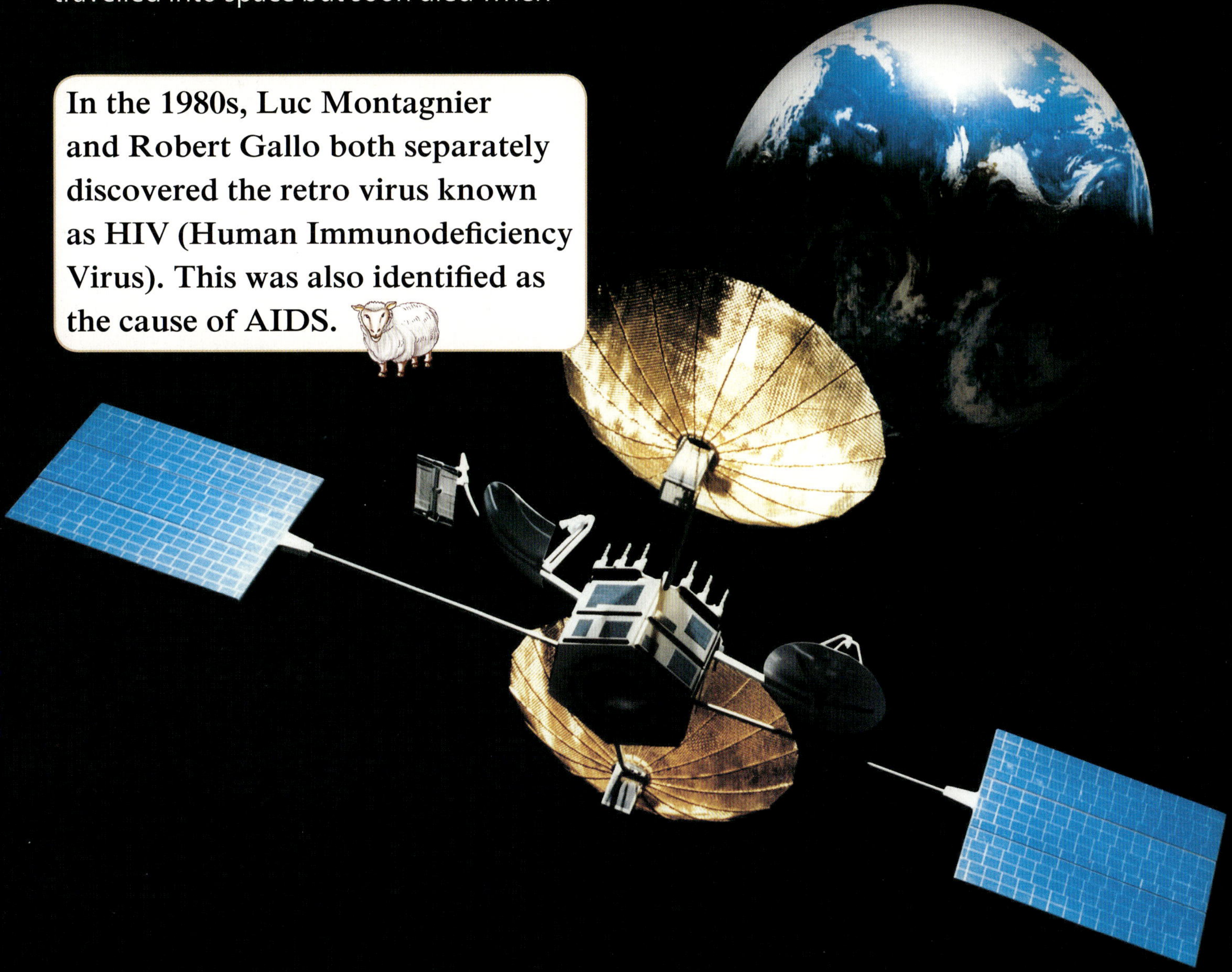

SCIENTIFIC BREAKTHROUGH

The first photograph

Joseph Niepce

Niepce placed an engraving onto a metal plate coated in bitumen and then exposed it to light. The shadowy areas of the engraving blocked light, but the whiter areas permitted light to react with the chemicals on the plate. When Niepce placed the metal plate in a solvent, gradually an image, until then invisible, appeared. However, Niepce's photograph required eight hours of light exposure to be created and after appearing, would soon fade away.

A building photograph taken by Joseph Niepce in 1826 is known as the world's First Photograph but actually this is the earliest surviving photograph. This was captured by an eight-hour light exposure onto the plate to get the image. This over exposure resulted in sunlight on both sides of the building.

It represents the view of the courtyard of Niepce's house at Gras, France, taken from the window of his workroom. On the left side of the image is the pigeon-house and to the right of it is a pear-tree with a patch of sky showing through an opening in the branches. In the centre of the image is the slanting roof of the barn; the long building behind it is the bake house, with chimney. On the right side of the image is another wing of the house.

The first photographic image

An 1909, Wilbur wright photographed the town of Centrocelli, Italy producing the first aerial photographs taken from an aeroplane.

Evolution of photography and its elements

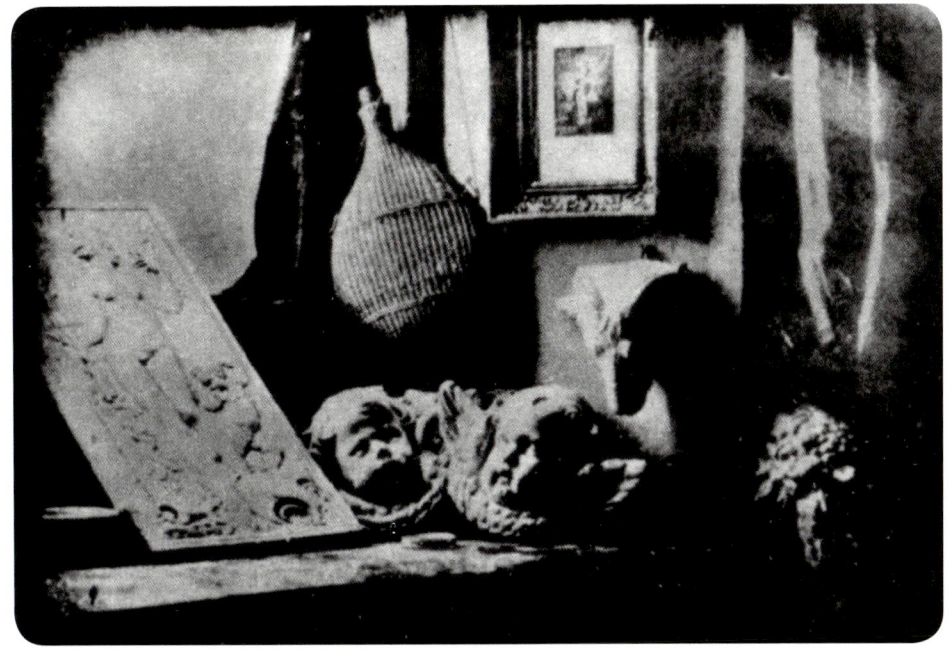
Daguerreotype

> Archimedes, a prolific ancient Greek mathematician invented the water screw, a device for raising water using an encased screw open at both ends.

Louis Daguerre was the inventor of the first practical process of photography. In 1829, he formed a partnership with Niepce to improve the process he had developed.

In 1839 after several years of experimentation and Niepce's death, Daguerre developed a more convenient and effective method of photography, naming it after himself - **the daguerreotype**.

The inventor of the first negative from which multiple positive prints were made was Henry Fox Talbot, an English botanist and mathematician and a contemporary of Daguerre.

Talbot sensitized paper to light with a silver salt solution. He then exposed the paper to light. The background became black, and the subject was rendered in gradations of grey. This was a negative image, and from the paper negative, Talbot made contact prints, reversing the light and shadows to create a detailed picture. In 1841, he perfected this paper-negative process. The new process was called the calotype, from the Greek kalos, meaning 'beautiful'.

SCIENTIFIC BREAKTHROUGH

Tintypes, patented in 1856 by Hamilton Smith, were another medium that heralded the birth of photography. A thin sheet of iron was used to provide a base for light-sensitive material, yielding a positive image.

In 1851, Frederick Scoff Archer, an English sculptor, invented the wet plate negative. Using a viscous solution of collodion, he coated glass with light-sensitive silver salts. As it was glass and not paper, this wet plate created a more stable and detailed negative.

Photography advanced considerably when sensitized materials could be coated on plate glass. However, wet plates had to be developed quickly before the emulsion dried. In the field, this meant carrying along a portable darkroom.

The first flexible roll films, dates back to 1889 were made of cellulose nitrate which is chemically similar to guncotton. A nitrate-based film deteriorates over time and releases harmful gases. It is also highly flammable. Thus, special storage for these types of films is required.

> **Cellophane is a thin, transparent, waterproof protective film that is used in many types of packaging. It was invented in 1908 by Jacques Edwin Brandenberger, a Swiss chemist.**

Evolution of photography and its elements

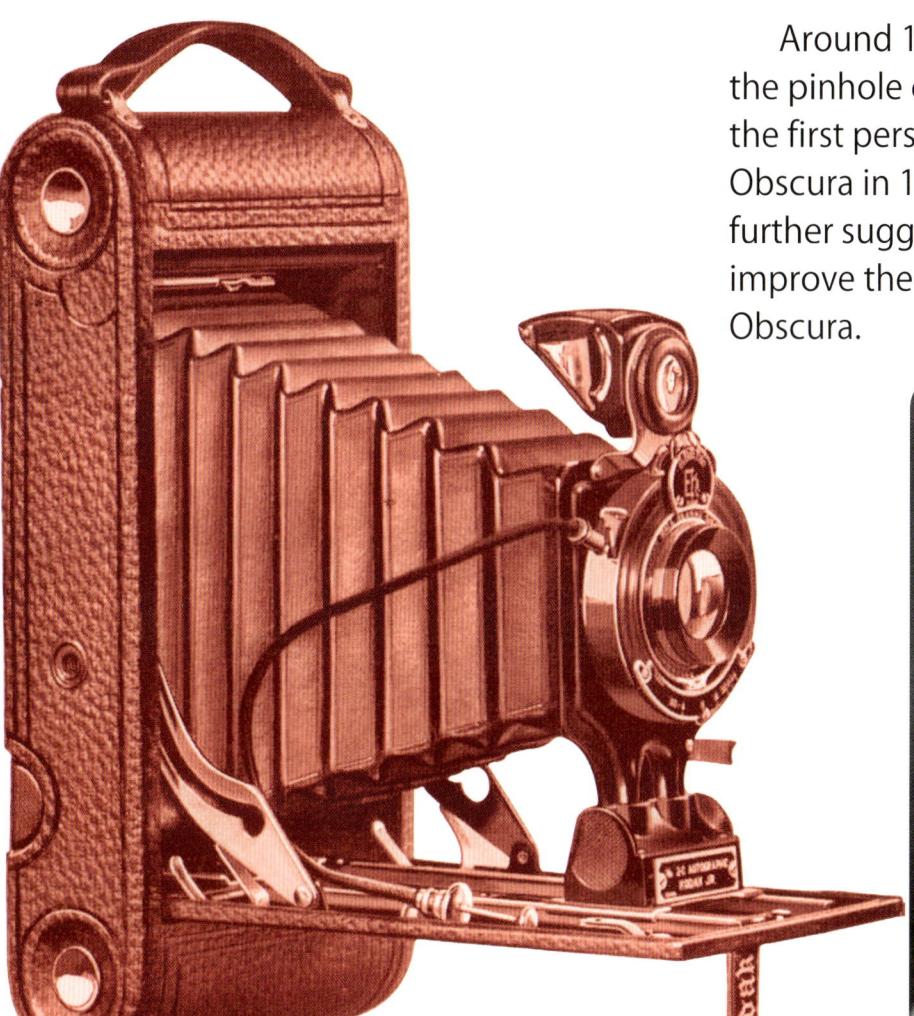

Around 1600, Della Porta reinvented the pinhole camera. Johannes Kepler was the first person to coin the phrase Camera Obscura in 1604, and in 1609, Kepler further suggested the use of a lens to improve the image projected by a Camera Obscura.

George Eastman

Nitrate film is historically important because it was used for the development of roll films. The first flexible movie film measured 35-mm wide and came in long rolls on a spool. In the mid-1920s, using this technology, 35-mm roll film was developed for the camera. By the late 1920s, medium-format roll film was created. It measured six centimetres wide and had a paper backing making it easy to handle in daylight. This led to the development of the twin-lens-reflex camera in 1929.

George Eastman, a dry plate manufacturer from Rochester, New York, invented the Kodak camera. For $22.00, an amateur could purchase a camera with enough film for 100 shots.

SCIENTIFIC BREAKTHROUGH

In 1879, the dry plate was invented, a glass negative plate with a dried gelatin emulsion. Dry plates could be stored for a period of time. Photographers no longer needed portable darkrooms and could now hire technicians to develop their photographs. Dry processes absorbed light so rapidly that the hand-held camera was now possible.

In 1889, George Eastman invented film with a base that was flexible, unbreakable and could be rolled. Emulsions coated on a cellulose nitrate film base, such as Eastman's, made the mass-produced box camera a reality.

Polaroid photography was invented by Edwin Herbert Land. Land was the American inventor and physicist whose one-step process for developing and

Edwin Herbert Land

printing photos created instant photography. The first Polaroid camera was sold to the public in November, 1948.

Fuji introduced the disposable camera in 1986. In 1984, Canon demonstrated the first digital electronic still camera.

12

The first test tube baby

On July 25, 1978, Louise Joy Brown, the world's first successful 'test-tube baby' was born in Great Britain. Though the technology that made her conception possible was heralded as a triumph in medicine and science, many feared that it would be ill-used in future.

Brown was born to Lesley and John Brown, who had been trying to conceive for nine years, but without success because of Lesley's blocked fallopian tubes. On November 10, 1977, Lesley underwent in vitro fertilization (IVF) procedure. Dr. Steptoe took an egg from one of her ovaries and Dr Edwards mixed that egg with John's sperm into a special solution. The fertilized egg was successfully embedded into Lesley's uterus wall.

Louise Joy Brown was born at 11:47 p.m., through a planned caesarean section delivered by Dr. John Webster, an obstetrician and gynaecologist at Oldham General Hospital, Oldham. She weighed 2.608 kg at birth. Her younger sister, Natalie Brown, was also conceived through IVF, four years later, and became the world's fortieth IVF baby and the first one to give birth herself—naturally—in 1999.

Anders Celsius (1701-1744) was a Swedish professor of astronomy who devised the Celsius thermometer.

SCIENTIFIC BREAKTHROUGH

The first cloned animal

Dolly was the first mammal cloned from the DNA of an adult animal. She was a Finn Dorset sheep born in 1996 and was hailed as a monumental scientific breakthrough when her birth was announced in early 1997. Scientists at Scotland's Roslin Institute used somatic cell nuclear transfer (SCNT), a reproductive cloning method, to produce the lamb, which carried the same nuclear DNA as the donor sheep (the cells were taken from the donor's udders). Dolly made headlines around the world and launched a public debate about the possibilities and ethics of cloning. Over the years, research groups around the world reported the cloning of mice, rats, cows, goats, rabbits, pigs, a horse, a mule and a dog.

In 2003 Dolly was put to sleep. Though she lived only about half the expected 10 to 12 years life span for a Finn Dorset sheep, scientists who conducted a post-mortem examination of her found that other than her ailments (arthritis and lung cancer), she appeared to be normal. The celebrity sheep was the mother of six lambs, which were brought into the world in the old-fashioned way.

The first computer

A historian might tell you that the first computer was the abacus, which was invented in Asia about 5000 years ago. However, the first modern computer was actually invented during World War II when a team of scientists and engineers at the University of Pennsylvania invented a general-purpose electronic digital calculator known as ENIAC (Electronic Numerator, Integrator, Analyzer, and Computer).

It consisted of 18,000 vacuum tubes and it was capable of adding 5,000 ten-digit decimal numbers per second. It also contained 7,200 crystal diodes, 1,500 relays, 70,000 resistors, 10,000 capacitors and around 5 million hand-soldered joints. It weighed approximately 30 short tons, took up about 1800 square feet (167 m^2), and consumed 150 kW of power.

It was the first large-scale, electronic, digital computer capable of being reprogrammed so that it could solve a variety of computing problems. The ENIAC was originally designed to calculate artillery firing tables for the U.S. Army's Ballistics Research Laboratory. However, some of the first problems that were run on the ENIAC were related to the design of the hydrogen bomb. The ENIAC was definitely a revolutionary development, which at that time was far ahead of any other calculators.

SCIENTIFIC BREAKTHROUGH

The first computer mouse

The computer mouse as we know it today was invented and developed by Douglas Englebart during the 60's and was patented on November 17, 1970. While creating the mouse, Douglas was working at the Stanford Research Institute and originally referred to the mouse as a 'X-Y Position Indicator for a Display System'. This mouse was first used with the Xerox Alto computer system in 1973. However, because of its lack of success the first widely used mouse is credited to being the mouse found on the Apple Lisa computer. Today, the mouse is found and used on every computer.

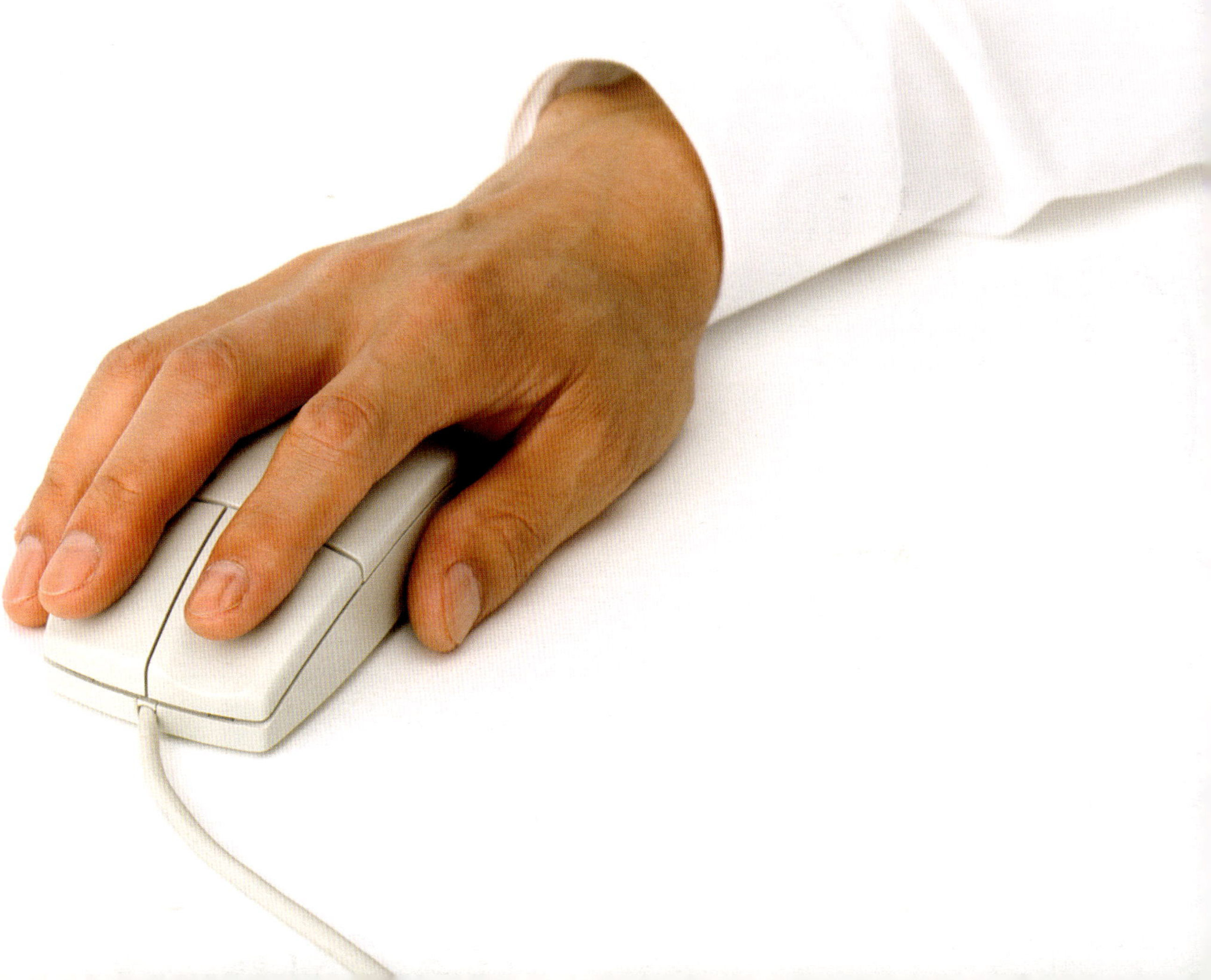

The first motorcycle

American, Sylvester Howard Roper (1823-1896) invented a two-cylinder, steam-engine motorcycle (powered by coal) in 1867. This is considered as the first motorcycle.

A German called Gottlieb Daimler invented the first gas-engine motorcycle in 1885, which was an engine attached to a wooden bike. This invention marked the integration of the development of a viable gas-powered engine and the modern bicycle.

Gottlieb Daimler

Designed and built by the German inventors Gottlieb Daimler and Wilhelm Maybach in Bad Cannstatt (Stuttgart) in 1885, it was essentially a motorised bicycle. The inventors called their invention the **Reitwagen** ('riding car'). It was also the first petroleum-powered vehicle.

SCIENTIFIC BREAKTHROUGH

The first X-Ray

Wilhelm Rontgen, a German physicist accidentally discovered X-rays when he was conducting experiments with the radiation from cathode rays. He noticed that the rays were able to penetrate opaque black paper wrapped around a cathode ray tube, causing a nearby table to glow with florescence. He also found that the new ray would pass through most substances casting shadows of solid objects on pieces of film. He named the new ray X-ray because in mathematics 'X' denotes the unknown quantity. Soon after he used a photographic plate and had his wife, Bertha, placed her hand in the path of the X-rays, creating the world's first X-ray picture. The news of Roentgen's discovery spread quickly throughout the world. In early 1896, X-rays began to be utilized clinically in the United States for capturing images of bone fractures and gunshot wounds. In 1901 Wilhelm Rontgen was awarded the very first Nobel Prize in Physics for this discovery.

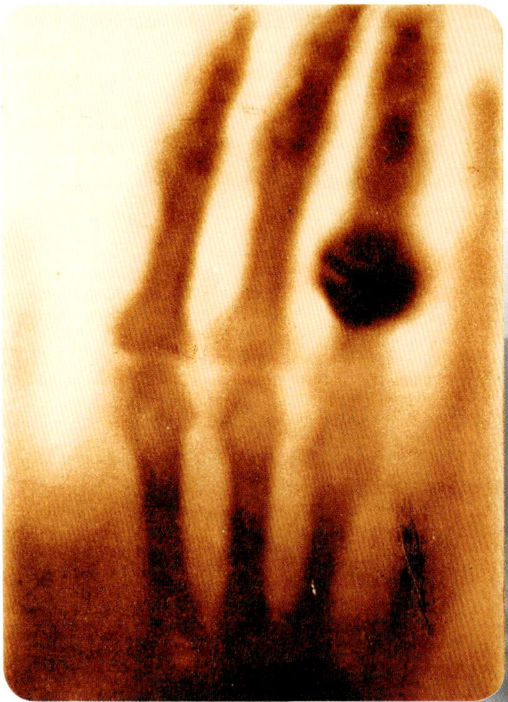

Wilhelm Rontgen

The first microprocessor

A microprocessor, or a logic chip, is a computer processor on a microchip. It is an assembly of all the integrated circuits (ICs) to perform most of the functions of a computer's central processing unit (CPU).

In November, 1971, a company called Intel publicly introduced the world's first single chip microprocessor, the Intel 4004. It was invented by Intel engineers Federico Faggin, Ted Hoff, and Stan Mazor. After the invention of integrated circuits revolutionized computer design, the only place to go down was size of the processing unit. The Intel 4004 chip took the integrated circuit down one step further by placing all the parts that made a computer think (that is, central processing unit, memory, input and output controls) on one small chip. Programming intelligence into inanimate objects had now become possible.

> Lord Kelvin designed the Kelvin scale, in which 0 K is defined as absolute zero and the size of one degree is the same as the size of one degree Celsius.

SCIENTIFIC BREAKTHROUGH

Aspirin— the miracle drug

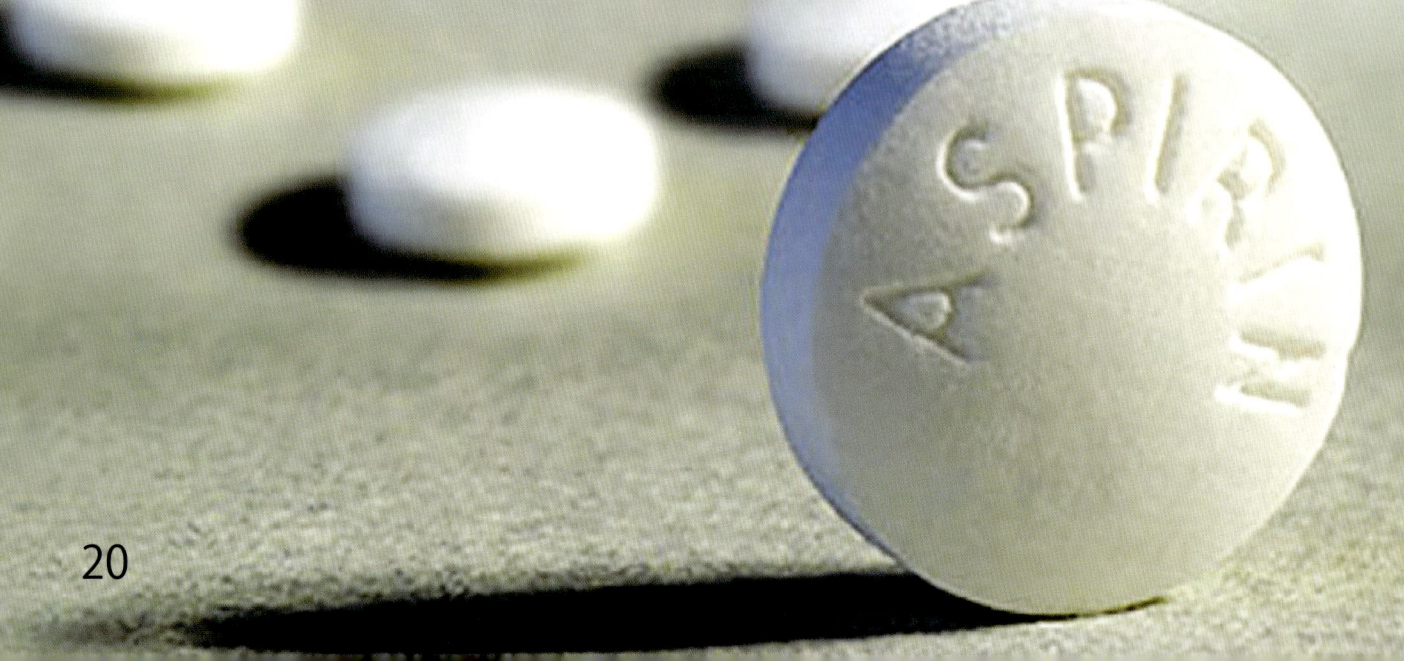

Aspirin is so familiar that you don't even notice it in the medicine cabinet until you have a headache. Yet this little white pill was one of the first wonder drugs to be developed during modern times. Simple but surprisingly complex, researchers are still discovering the health-giving benefits of aspirin. First recorded in ancient Greece, a simple herbal remedy became a rock star in pharmacology around 1900.

The use of extracts made from the willow tree for pain management can be traced back to ancient times. The active ingredient in willow bark was extracted by Johann Buchner, in 1828, which he called salicin. In 1829, Henri Leroux extracted salicin in crystalline form for the first time. Raffaele Piria succeeded in obtaining the salicin in its pure state and called it 'salicylic acid'. The salicylic acid was tough on stomachs. This made scientists search for a means to neutralize it. The first person to do so was a French chemist, Charles Frederic Gerhardt. In 1853, Gerhardt neutralized salicylic acid by sodium and acetyl chloride, creating acetylsalicylic acid. Gerhardt's product was a great success but he abandoned his discovery as he had no desires to market it.

In 1899, Felix Hoffmann, rediscovered Gerhardt's formula. He gave it to his father who was suffering from the pain of arthritis. He found the drug very promising and convinced a German company called Bayer to market the new wonder drug. Aspirin was first sold as a powder and then, in 1915, the first Aspirin tablets were made.

Aspirin—the miracle drug

ASPIRIN

Tablets mit 500 mg Acetylsalicylsaure

20 Tablets

Aspirin has been an important pain reliever since prehistoric times. At the dawn of modern medicine as the Western world knows it in the early 1800s, further refinements converted the ancient willow tea extract into a prosaic pill. With the rise of international corporations in the early 1900s, the homely aspirin became a money maker for the German drug and dye giant Bayer.

Aspirin has done miracles in the Spanish flu epidemic in 1918. It became extremely popular in the early part of the twentieth century. Generic version of Aspirin flooded American markets after Bayer's American patent of Aspirin expired in 1917. Aspirin continued to be the king of analgesics for half a century until it lost the war to advanced analgesics like paracetamol, which was introduced in 1956 and ibuprofen introduced in 1969.

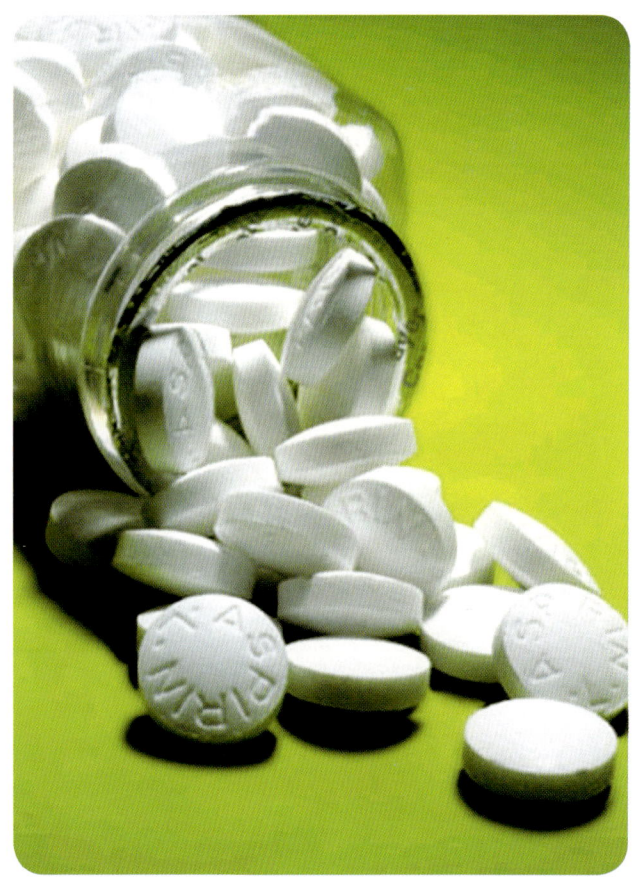

SCIENTIFIC BREAKTHROUGH

Penicillin—the first antibiotic

Alexander Fleming

Penicillin was discovered accidentally by Dr Alexander Fleming while working at St. Mary's Hospital in London. He was examining a culture of **Staphylococcus aureus**, a pathogenic bacterium when he noticed that it had been contaminated by a mold. He observed that species of the mold was inhibiting the bacterial growth. He took a sample of the mold and characterized it. He found that it belonged to penicillium family and could treat many types of harmful bacterial infections. Later, he named it penicillin and reported his findings in 1929. However, penicillin, the first antibiotic, was purified by Howard Florey and Ernst Chain during the Second World War. This discovery revolutionized the medicinal research and was recognized as the greatest advances in therapeutics. Fleming along with Florey and Chain received a Nobel Prize in 1945 for their discovery which led to the development of lifesaving antibiotics.

Ernst Chain

Howard Florey

ARPANET—the beginning of Internet

Internet is the network of networks which connects computer systems worldwide by various means such as telephone wires or satellites. The www (**World Wide Web**) is a network of sites that can be searched and retrieved by a special procedure known as a Hypertext Transfer protocol (HTTP). This protocol searches the address on the web servers and automatically retrieves the saved information for viewing.

The Internet technology was developed by Vinton Cerf in 1973 as part of a United States Department of Defense Advanced Research Projects Agency (DARPA) project. The computer network this project produced was called **ARPANET** that linked U.S. scientific and academic researchers.

ARPA scientists, working closely with experts in Stanford, developed a common language that would allow different networks to communicate with each other. This was known as a transmission control protocol/internet protocol (TCP/IP). Further developments in technology and World Wide Web, released the internet for everyone in 1991.

ADDRESS @ http://www.arpanet

Water purification

Humans have been storing and distributing water for centuries. The Greeks were among the first to gain an interest in water quality. They used aeration basins for water purification. The Romans were the first to construct water distribution networks in history. They used river, spring or groundwater for provisioning.

The first municipal water treatment plant for drinking water was built in Paisley, Scotland in 1804 by John Gibb, to supply drinking water to the entire city. This plant consisted of concentric sand and gravel filters, and its distribution system consisted of a horse and cart. In 1806, Paris operated a large water treatment plant where water was stored for 12 hours and filtered before supply. Filters consisted of sand and charcoal and were replaced every six hours.

In 1807, Glasgow, Scotland, was one of the first cities to pipe filtered water to consumers. By 1827, slow sand filters designed by Robert Thom were common in Scotland homes for drinking water purification. Similar systems were designed by James Simpson in London. Thom's filters were cleaned by backwash, while Simpson's required scraping. The Simpson design eventually became the famous English model throughout the world.

> Jean Bernard Léon Foucault, a French physicist, invented the gyroscope in 1852.

Water purification

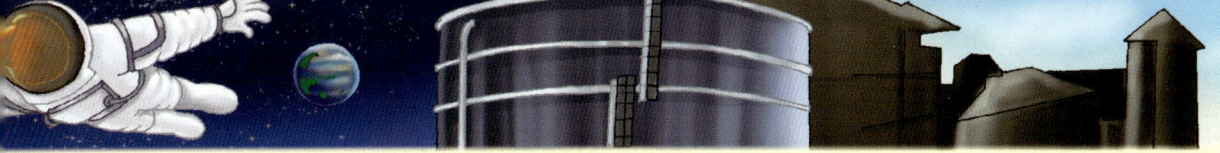

The drinking water, contaminated with microbes, can lead to a miserable bout of stomach pain and loose bowels, and a hasty trip to a local medical clinic. The World Health Organization reported that water borne diseases are the world's leading cause of death, claiming more number of deaths than the war, terrorism and weapons of mass destruction combined together. Children in impoverished countries, whose immune systems are weakened by malnutrition and other stresses, are particularly at higher risk. The condition used to be even worse in earlier times. For centuries, even in developed countries, mysterious periodic outbreaks of water-borne cholera regularly killed many thousands of people.

In 1854, British scientist John Snow found that the disease was caused by microorganisms in sewage that contaminated the water supply. He came up with the idea to add chlorine to the water. This practise successfully killed the microorganisms, and the illness rate plummeted. Since then, more chemical and filtration technologies have been developed to make our drinking water safe.

SCIENTIFIC BREAKTHROUGH

Robot

A robot is generally a machine in the form of a human that can perform functions attributed to the humans. It is a reprogrammable, multifunctional manipulator designed to move material, parts, tools or specialized devices through various programmed motions for the performance of a variety of tasks. Karel Capek is credited for the first use of the word 'robot'. In 1956, George C. Devol and Joseph F. Engelberger made a serious and commercially successful effort to develop a real, working robot. They persuaded Norman Schafler of Condec Corporation in Danbury that they had the basis of a commercial success. Engelberger started a manufacturing company 'Unimation' which stood for universal automation. In this way, the first commercial company to make robots was established. Their first robot was nicknamed the 'Unimate'. For his achievements in the field of robotics, Engelberger is known as the 'father of robotics'. The first Unimate robot was installed at the General Motors plant to work with heated die-casting machines. Most of the initial Unimates were sold to extract die castings and to perform spot welding on auto bodies, both tasks being particularly hateful jobs for people.

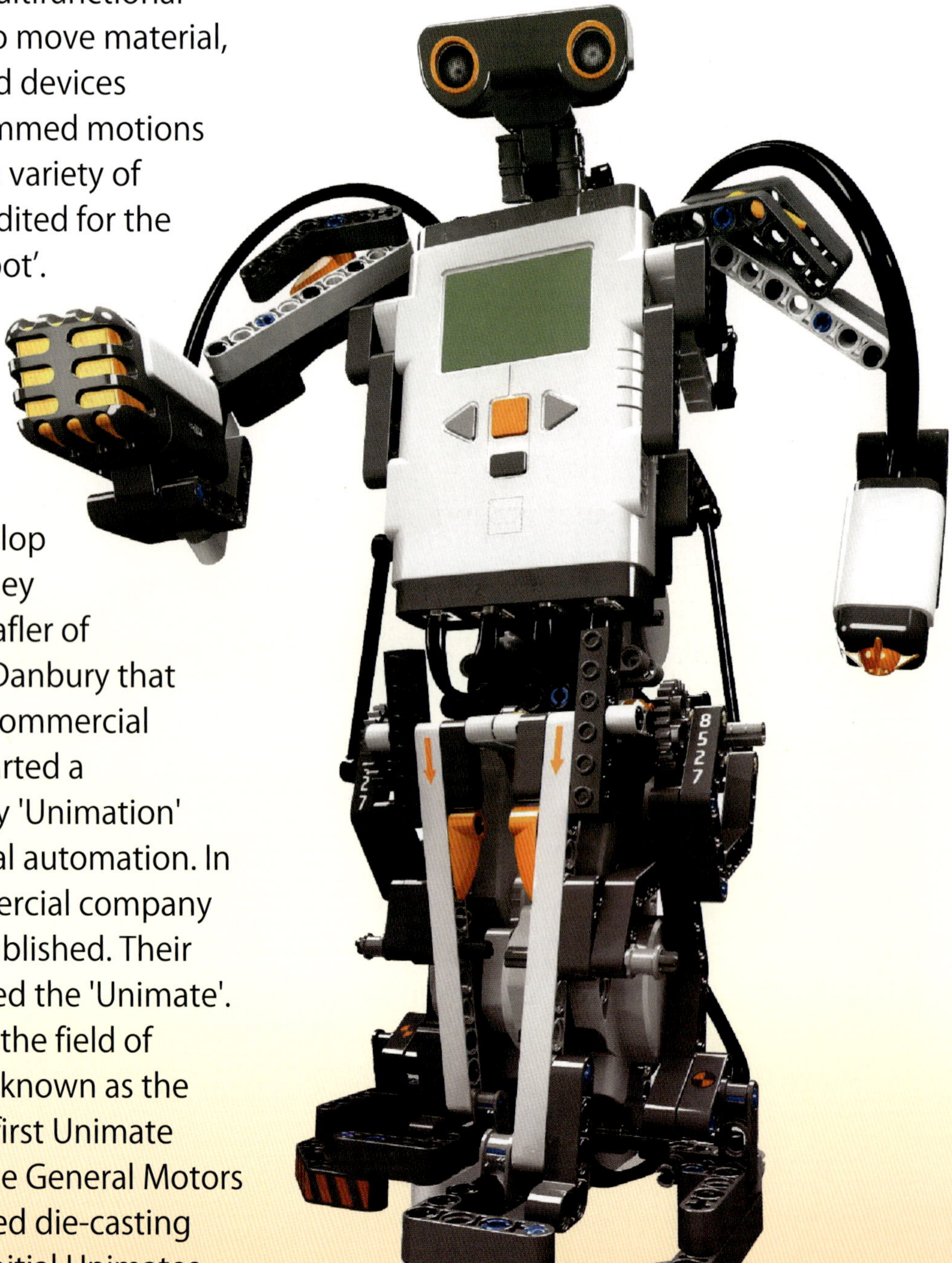

26

Artificial limb

A limb or joint lost through accident, disease or birth defect maybe replaced with an artificial limb or joint. Such a replacement is called **prosthesis** from the Latin word meaning 'addition'. Crude artificial limbs have been used since the earliest loss of an arm, leg, hand or foot.

The modern era of artificial limbs began with the famous French surgeon Ambroise Pare (1517-1590; considered the 'father of modern surgery'). Pare began his career as a barber-surgeon. In 1536 he became a battlefield surgeon. On the battleground his greatest challenge was developing ways to deal with gunshot wounds. The devastating nature of these wounds meant that the soldiers' limbs often had to be amputated. After devising safer, more effective methods of amputation, Pare turned his attention to the design of artificial limbs to replace the ones he had surgically removed.

An artificial hand made by Pare had fingers that moved individually by means of tiny internal cogs and levers. When amputating a limb, Pare tried to leave enough stump so that it could be fitted with an artificial limb. Because of Pare's eminence, his ideas and designs for prostheses (plural of the word prosthesis) or artificial limbs became well-known.

Ambroise Pare

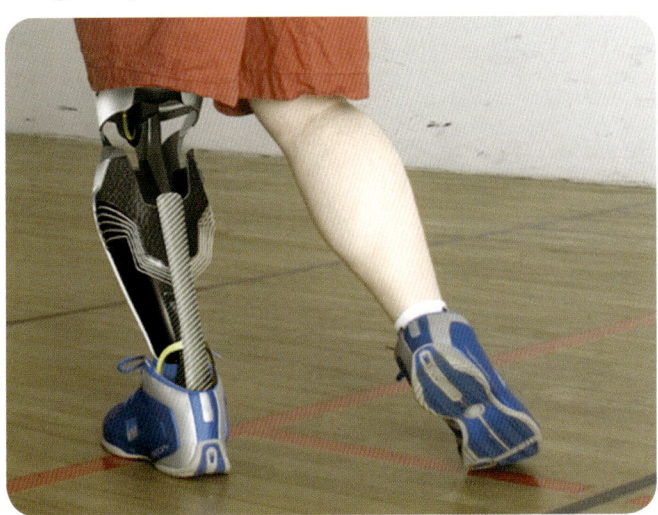

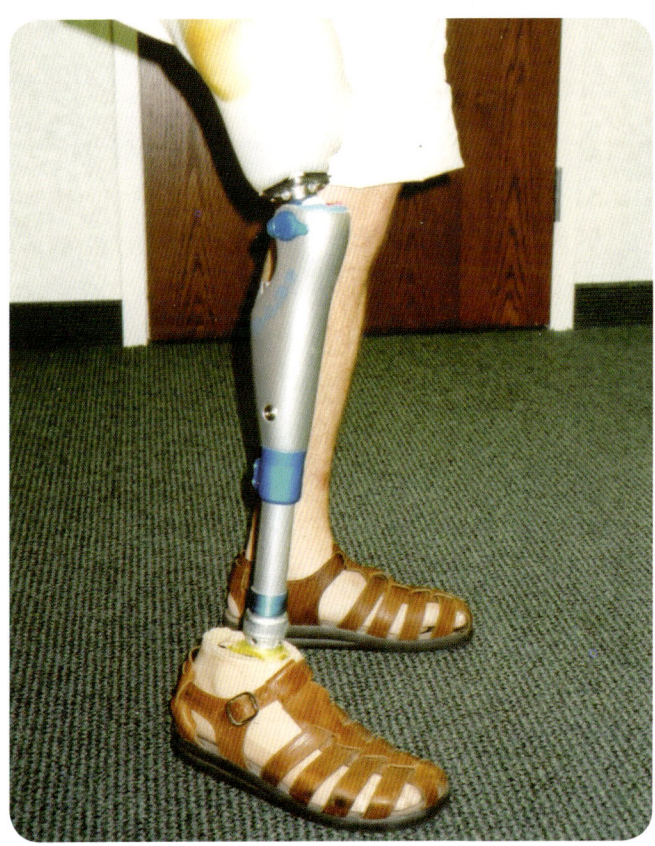

SCIENTIFIC BREAKTHROUGH

The first vaccine—Smallpox vaccination

Edward Jenner

For many centuries, smallpox devastated mankind. In modern times we do not have to worry about it thanks to the remarkable work of Edward Jenner and later developments from his endeavours. In 1796, he invented the smallpox vaccination. Dr Jenner was aware of the belief that anybody who contracted cowpox, never contracted smallpox. He realized that inoculating people with cowpox would immunize them against smallpox. He researched this issue and performed a test to confirm his hypothesis. He inoculated an eight-year-old boy with matter taken from a cowpox pustule. The matter was taken from the hand of Sarah Nelmes, who had caught the disease from a cow named Blossom. Phipps developed coxpox and quickly recovered. Several weeks later, the boy was inoculated with smallpox, and did not contract the disease. And so, Dr Jenner created history and saved humanity from the deadly enemy called Smallpox.

> **Karl Gothe Jansky was an American radio engineer who pioneered and developed radio astronomy. In 1932, he detected the first radio waves from a cosmic source —the central region of the Milky Way Galaxy.**

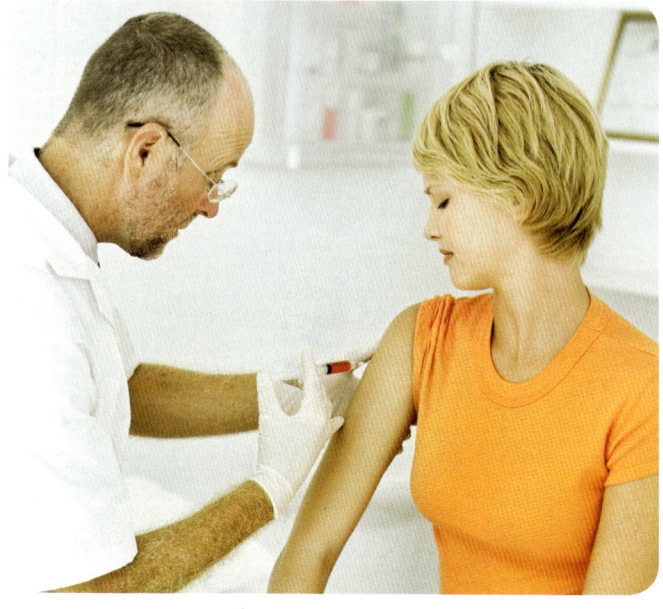

Open-heart surgery

Opening the chest to operate directly on an exposed heart is major surgery. For many years the procedure was considered impossible because performing the operation would cause the heart to stop beating. A few pioneers, however, did perform emergency surgery directly on the open heart. One of the first was African-American surgeon Daniel Hale Williams. Williams opened the chest of a stabbed victim and sewed up the pericardium (the sac surrounding the heart) in 1893.

An American surgeon named John H. Gibbon Jr. devoted himself to solving this problem in the 1930s. Assisted by his wife Mary, Gibbon developed a workable pump-

Daniel Hale Williams

oxygenator in 1931. This heart-lung machine switched blood from the veins through a catheter (a slender tube) to a machine. The machine supplied the blood with oxygen and then pumped the blood back into the arteries. In 1953, Gibbon ushered in the era of open-heart surgery by using his heart-lung machine on a patient suffering from heart failure.

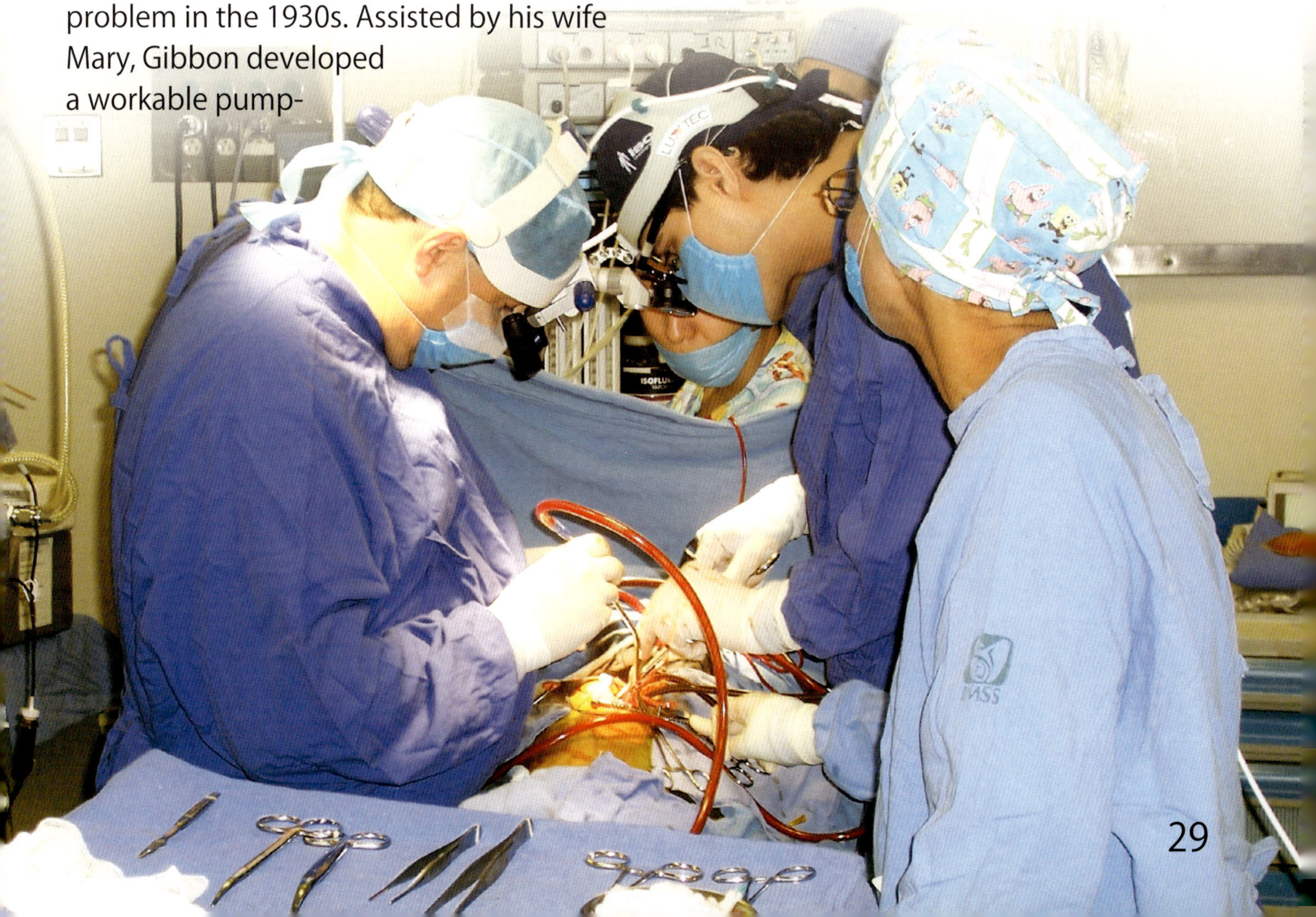

SCIENTIFIC BREAKTHROUGH

The human genome

The genome consists of all the hereditary information of an organism. This information is passed through generations and is encoded by Deoxyribonucleic acid (DNA). The human genome is stored on 23 chromosome pairs. The one pair is sex-determining and remaining twenty two are autosomal chromosome pairs.

The Human Genome Project (HGP) was one of the great feats of exploration in history— an inward voyage of discovery rather than an outward exploration of the planet or the cosmos. It was an international research effort to sequence and map all of the human genes together, known as the human genome. Completed in April 2003, the HGP gave us the ability to, for the first time, to read nature's complete genetic blueprint for building a human being.

The HGP has revealed that the size of the human genome is about 109 base pairs and there are probably about 20,500 human genes. The completed human sequence can now identify their locations. This ultimate product of the HGP has given the world a resource of detailed information about the structure, organization and function of the complete set of human genes. This information can be thought of as the basic set of inheritable 'instructions' for the development and function of a human being.

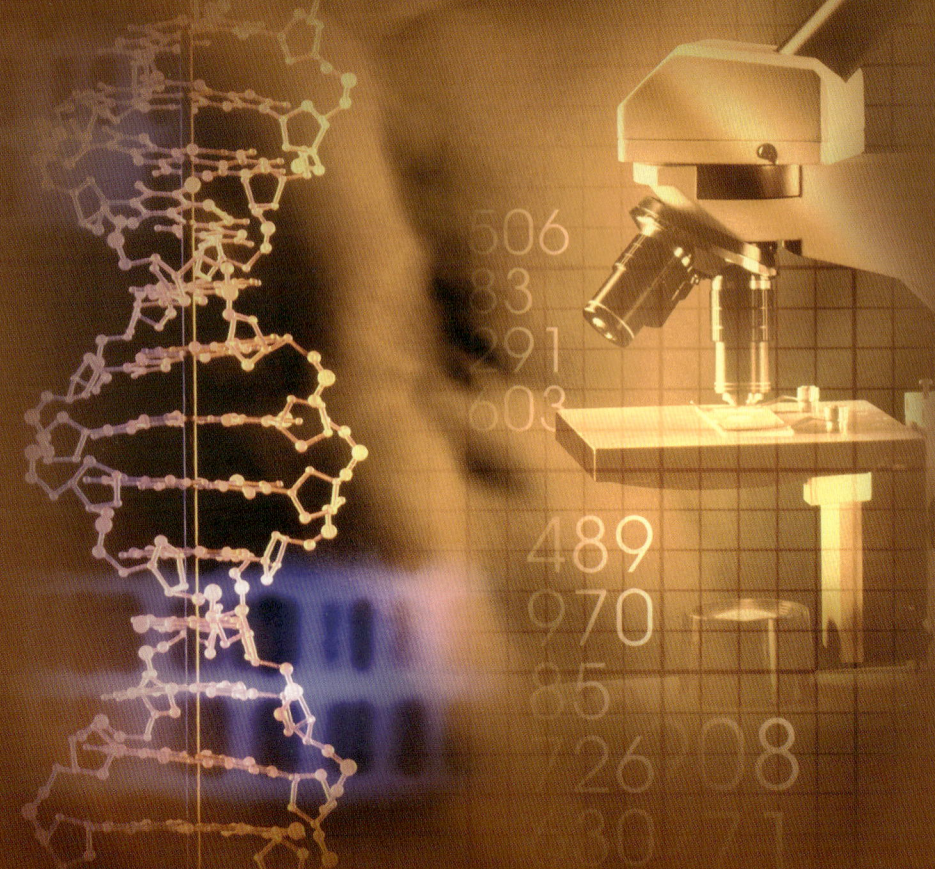

Test Your MEMORY

1. Which spacecraft made the first safe landing on the moon?

2. When was the first motorbike invented?

3. How did the process of photography evolve?

4. When was the first photograph taken?

5. What was the ARPANET?

6. What is aspirin used for?

7. Who invented the first microscope?

8. When was the first animal cloned?

9. Name the first antibiotic drug.

10. Who invented the first robot?

11. Who did the first successful open heart surgery?

12. What is the size of human genome?

SCIENTIFIC BREAKTHROUGH

Index

A
abacus 15
Alexander Fleming 22
Ambroise Pare 27
analgesics 21
antibiotic 22
Aspirin 20, 21

B
Bayer 20, 21
box camera 12
Buzz Aldrin 5

C
cathode rays 18
cellulose nitrate 10, 12
Charles Frederic Gerhardt 20
Cholera 25
Christiaan Barnard 3
cloning 14
Cowpox 28

D
Daniel Hale Williams 29
Diabetes 3
Douglas Englebart 16

E
Edward Jenner 28
Edwin Herbert Land 12
ENIAC 15
Ernst Chain 22

F
fallopian tubes 13
Felix Hoffmann 20
Frederick Scoff Archer 10

G
gelatin emulsion 12
Gottlieb Daimler 17

H
Hamilton Smith 10
Henri Leroux 20
Henry Fox Talbot 9
Howard Florey 22
human genome 30

I
ibuprofen 21
integrated circuits 19
in vitro fertilization 13

J
James Simpson 24
Johannes Kepler 11
Joseph Niepce 8

K
Karel Capek 26

L
Louis Daguerre 9
Louise Joy Brown 13

M
Marius Barnard 3

Michael Collins 5

N
Neil Armstrong 5
Nobel Prize 18, 22

P
Penicillin 22
Pneumonia 3
prosthesis 27

R
radio transmitter 6
Reitwagen 17
Robert Thom 24
robot 26

S
salicin 20
salicylic acid 20
satellite 6, 7
Smallpox 28
Sylvester Howard Roper 17

T
thermometer 6, 13

V
vaccination 28
vacuum tubes 15
veins 29

W
Wilhelm Rontgen 18
World Health Organization 25